D. J. SMITH

*Discovering*
# Horse-drawn Commercial Vehicles

SHIRE PUBLICATIONS LTD

# Contents

Introduction                                          3

1. Early history of horse transport                   4

2. From 1500 to the nineteenth century                9

3. Delivery vehicles                                 20

4. Public utility and special vehicles               32

5. American types                                    61

6. Features and methods of construction              65

7. Driving and harness                               71

8. Where to see horse-drawn commercial vehicles      74

Glossary                                             76

Bibliography                                         78

Index                                                79

ACKNOWLEDGEMENTS
The author acknowledges with thanks the help received from the
following: B. B. Murdock; R. A. Brown OBE; Marylian Watney; the
Curator and staff of the Hereford and Worcester County Museum; C.
P. Atkins, the Librarian of the National Railway Museum; the staff of
Leicester Museums; staff of the Midland Counties Dairy Ltd; the
London Harness Horse Parade Society.
    Line drawings by the author.
    Photographs are acknowledged as follows: K. Bennett, plate 15;
GWR photograph, plate 27; HDV Series, photograph CWS, plates 9,
11, 13, 17, 18, 19; HDV Series, photograph B. B. Murdock, plates 4, 6,
8, 10, 12, 16, 20, 21, 26; HDV Series, photograph Savage's, plate 32; A.
Hustwitt, plates 2, 3, 22, 23, 25; Cadbury Lamb, plate 5; Leicester
Transport Museum, plates 7, 31; St Albans City Museum, plate 1.

Cover photograph of Windsor Horse Show by Cadbury Lamb.

British Library Cataloguing in Publication data available.

Printed in Great Britain by C. I. Thomas & Sons (Haverfordwest) Ltd,
Press Buildings, Merlins Bridge, Haverfordwest.

# Introduction

Despite a revived interest in early transport, horse-drawn commercial and utility vehicles tend to be neglected or considered unworthy of serious study. The purpose of this book is to foster interest in a subject which, though not perhaps as romantic as the elegant coach or carriage, is equally rewarding. It is undeniable that the use of cart, wagon and van has played an integral part in the development of modern civilisation. There are even indications that there may be a revival of horse transport, in a more than limited sense, due to the increasing cost of motor vehicles and vagaries of the fuel crisis. While it is impossible that horses will ever replace mechanical traction for more than local usage, time and motion study experts have several times proved their superiority for deliveries within a few miles of base or depot. It is also certain that a brewer's dray, drawn by a team of willing horses, is more of an eye-catcher than the most impressive motor vehicle and thus a better medium for advertising and publicity, a fact of which an increasing number of commercial concerns and public utilities are now becoming aware.

It should be noted, in studying this subject, that many people confuse the terms *cart* and *wagon*. A cart is usually a two-wheeled vehicle, while a wagon has four wheels, although some types of lighter four-wheeled vehicles are often termed 'carts'. The layman often speaks of a coal cart and a water cart, both of which are more frequently four-wheeled. There is also confusion over the word *float*, especially since floats have been widely used for milk deliveries. Although literally meaning a low-slung two-wheeled vehicle, in modern terms the word is wrongly applied to all kinds of delivery vehicles, including four-wheeled semi-open vans and electric trucks.

Part of a chapter has been devoted to farm wagons and carts, which may be studied in greater detail in other books (see Bibliography). This has been necessary as vehicles for agricultural purposes form an important part of the development of more specialised commercial transport.

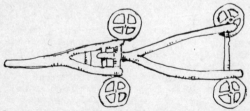

*Fig. 1. Double 'A' frame of early wagon, from a Scandinavian cave drawing.*

3

# 1. Early history of horse transport

### Early forms of wheeled transport

In prehistoric times, before the invention of the wheel, considerable use was made of the sledge or slide-car as a means of conveying burdens too cumbersome for pack animals or human porterage. The slide was made from branches of trees bound together with lengths of creeper or thongs of rawhide, eventually acquiring a basketwork container for the load. This would be raised slightly above ground level, the opposite end, corresponding with crude shafts, resting on either the shoulders of a man or the back of a draught animal.

The wheel is thought to have been invented in India or the Far East, at the dawn of history, although the exact date is unknown. Disc wheels may have been fitted to slides, thus forming a crude cart, before 3000 BC. This could have been drawn either by a single ox or by a pair of oxen, attached by means of a neck yoke based on a triangular or 'A' shaped framework. The wheel became fairly common in most countries of the Near and Middle East, gradually penetrating to Mediterranean Europe and finally to the rest of that continent.

Four-wheeled wagons, much later in developing, were at first mainly associated with ceremonial occasions and religious festivals. The early wagon, also with disc wheels, developed as a simple box structure on either an 'H' frame or a frame of double triangles (double 'A' shapes). There appear to have been four-wheeled vehicles in Crete before 1800 BC. Yet apart from the ceremonial significance it came to be recognised that, until recent years, two-wheeled carts were mainly used in highland districts while four-wheeled wagons developed on the central plains of Eurasia.

The horse was seldom employed as a beast of draught or burden during the early stages of transport history and was mainly used for warfare, ceremonial or sporting purposes. It was not until the time of the Roman Empire that horses were widely used to draw anything more substantial than two-wheeled hunting or war chariots. The ox-cart, however, was universal from the plains of the Ganges to the valley of the Nile and the steppes of central Asia. Draught connection was by means of a yoke attached to a central pole, the ox pushing with neck and shoulders against vertical bars of the yoke. Side shafts with neck harness began to develop with the increased use of horses and were fairly widespread, at least in Europe, from the fourth century AD. Neck collars were said to have been introduced from central Asia by nomadic tribes and better suited to the conformation of the draught horse than breast harness and pole draught, although this has been contested by experts, especially in military circles, for a

4

number of years. Shafts, although sometimes double or in pairs, were mainly used for single horses with smaller vehicles.

The earliest carriages and carts of both India and China are thought to have appeared between 2250 and 2000 BC. We learn of these from remains in burial places, from toys or models remaining almost intact, and from illustrations in contemporary art.

## Chinese developments

Chinese history, often confused with folklore and legend, attributes the invention of the wheel to a period directly before the Hsia Dynasty about 2000 BC. It is claimed that the Emperor Huang-ti was the inventor of both the solid wheel and the war chariot. His surname, 'Houan-yuan-shi', means 'from the family of the wagon pole'. He frequently led his clans to victory in chariots and is said to have conceived the idea of the wheel by watching the blossoms of a flower plucked from their stem and blown along the ground with circular motions.

During the Chu period from 1027 to 223 BC the Chinese had completed a network of internal roads and trade routes, supported by numerous inns or guest-houses. Roads were classed as suitable for pedestrians and horsemen, tracks for narrow-gauge vehicles, roads for broader vehicles, roads wide enough for wagons to pass in comfort, or three-lane highways broad enough for at least three of the largest wagons abreast. At a later period certain routes were reserved for high-ranking nobility and state officials and could not be profaned by ordinary people, most of whom were restricted to much rougher byways.

The first carts in China were developed from war chariots and used either for agricultural purposes or to supply the needs of an army in the field. A class of men known as carters or contractors

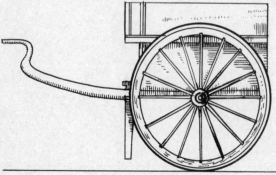

*Fig. 2. Chinese cart.*

flourished to supply the army with food, clothing and weapons of war, some owning hundreds of rude carts.

Models and sculpture from the Han dynasty show the use of both shafts and draught poles. These must have been the first commercial road vehicles in history, forerunners of the general service or bread and meat wagons of later years. It is interesting to note that wheels, either disc or spoked, were frequently large in proportion to the size of the vehicle on which they were mounted.

## The Greeks and Romans

While carts and wagons were introduced to the Greek islands through Crete, from the Near and Middle East, their development was greatly hampered by inferior roads and rough terrain. The Greeks traded by sea rather than by land and developed a civilisation in which simplicity and individual effort were considered virtues. Apart from chariots used for war and later sporting purposes, wheeled vehicles were little known. Those wishing to travel in wagons or carriages were considered self-indulgent or effeminate. Only the most primitive ox-wagons were used on farmland, of a type imitated by the Etruscans and Romans and later known as the *plaustrum*. This was a four-wheeled, flat-topped dray, first used for agriculture and later by city merchants.

The Romans had a wide range of vehicles for both commercial and military purposes, with equivalents of the carrier's cart, stage wagon, mail-coach and hackney cab. Their road system was unequalled for many centuries, although the vehicles themselves appear crude by later standards. They used oxen, horses and mules as their draught animals, although oxen would have been normally used for heavier vehicles and local journeys, rather than long-distance work. Roman civilisation in the eastern province of

*Fig. 3. Roman open wagon for wine barrel.*

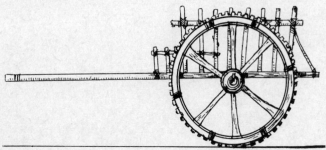

*Fig. 4. Medieval cart.*

Thrace, now known as Bulgaria, led to the invention of what appears to have been a slung or suspended carriage, which resembled a hammock on wheels. The territory of Pannonia (Hungary) was also rich in remains of carts and wagons from this period, as were the Celtic and some of the Scandinavian countries. It is probable that nomadic tribes from the heartland of central Asia used large numbers of vehicles in their migrations and indirectly influenced the design theories of dwellers on the plains of eastern and central Europe, with whom they may have had both close contacts and racial affinities.

## The Middle Ages

After the fall of the Roman Empire the greater part of Europe underwent a decline in material values and general standards of living. The fine road system built by the Romans fell into decay, and apart from rough tracks, unsuitable for any but mounted men, pedestrians or litters carried by pack animals, most transport was coastwise or by river barge. As among the ancient Greeks, healthy folk were expected to walk or ride on horseback, according to their means. The few litters or passenger vehicles available were reserved for the sick and elderly, although, in most cases, people were discouraged from travel and tended to live on self-sufficient country estates or in walled towns near navigable rivers. During the period known as the Middle Ages, from the widespread acceptance of Christianity until the Renaissance of the fifteenth century, there was near stagnation in the development of land transport. The Roman system of mail-coaches and a network of regular contacts between places of importance dwindled to a state of collapse and was not revived — on a universal scale — until comparatively modern times. The only form of improvement lay in the gradual acceptance of better harness, designed to respect the conformation of draught animals, approaching by slow degrees the standards of modern Europe, especially in the use of neck

7

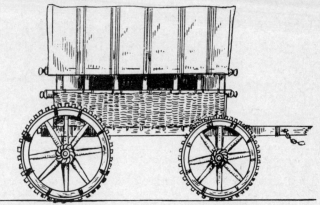

*Fig. 5. Medieval wagon with wicker sides.*

collars. The wagon with a perch or reinforced underbody, which may have been a Celtic innovation, thus distinguished from the perchless wagon of Asia, also became fairly widespread towards the end of the Middle Ages.

A typical cart or wagon of the late Middle Ages would have a floor of either planks or reinforced wickerwork. The sides would be semi-open in the form of staves or spindles, although some vehicles might be boarded up, especially the few needed for human transport, and headed (roofed over) with leather, felt or oilskins. The main items of freight would be timber and grain, while the main users of wagons were feudal lords and the monks of large monasteries. Some wagons had a slightly smaller pair of wheels at the front than the rear but most were equirotal (with all four wheels the same size). The outer rim of the wheel would be protected by iron studs, although later by strakes or hoops.

Towards the end of the Middle Ages military supply wagons were frequently used that could be converted into defence works, arranged in squares and circles not unlike the covered wagons of American settlers attacked by Red Indians. The Hussite general Prokop used wagons to great effect at the battle of Tachov, in which 3600 vehicles provided cover for his archers, by whom the knights of the Emperor Sigismond were soon defeated and put to flight. There is a popular German engraving of the fifteenth century showing an armed camp surrounded by both inner and outer circles of wagons, known as a wagon town or fortification, or *Wagenburg*. The Flemings were also adept at this style of warfare and designed a type of military wagon used by most European armies until the period of the Napoleonic wars.

## 2. From 1500 to the nineteenth century

### The carrier's wagon

The Renaissance period in Europe, from the fifteenth century onwards, saw great social and economic changes. The gradual ending of the feudal system and the improvement of agriculture, together with the increasing population of towns, led to farming for profit and the growth of commerce. Communities became interdependent rather than self-sufficient and travel was encouraged by all means available. Carts were improved and wagons used in greater numbers not only on the land, but also for the market and retail requirements of the growing towns.

The most advanced type of vehicle, especially from the sixteenth century, was the carrier's wagon, used for both passengers and produce. This was an enlarged version of the Flanders wagon and appears to have resembled a type fairly common in western Europe during this period. It usually had slightly larger wheels at the back than the front, with broad rims or tyres to smooth out ruts in the badly maintained roads. It was spindle-sided and may have been open-ended or provided with head and tail boards. Early wagons of this type carried about four tons but gradually increased in size so that by the seventeenth century they were able to carry at least double that amount. Each wagon would be drawn by a team of from ten to twelve horses, sometimes controlled by a man riding alongside on a nimble pony or cob. Regular journeys

*Fig. 6. Carrier's wagon, late eighteenth century.*

9

were made between London and the towns of the neighbouring counties carrying grain, fodder and general farm produce in one direction and returning with city produce, foreign imports and even ships' timbers from the yards of the London shipbuilders and breakers, which were widely used for building cottages and barns.

During the eighteenth century a version of the carrier's wagon, known as the **stage wagon** or 'poor man's stagecoach', carried both passengers and goods to all parts of the United Kingdom. Passengers were protected from the worst of the weather by a canvas cover supported on hoops or tilts, although they frequently had to walk up hills, to lighten the load. On many roads the jolting was so bad that trudging beside the vehicle would have been a welcome change after hours of crouching in a dark, stuffy interior. During the autumn and winter the roads were so bad that services had to be suspended for months at a time.

With improved roads, engineered towards the end of the eighteenth century by such men as Telford, Metcalf and McAdam, some vehicles owned by carriers became lighter and swifter. The carrier's cart of this period would be two-wheeled, usually covered or headed, to ply between villages until the coming of the motor van, although a limited number of the larger wagons were in general use until the end of the nineteenth century.

**Farm wagons**

The great land enclosures of the mid eighteenth century were a further incentive to agricultural improvements and the commercial growth they engendered. Farm wagons, especially for

*Fig. 7. Factory-made wagon.*

harvesting, were greatly improved and assumed the forms with which they were associated until the factory production of the late Victorian era. Most vehicles of this type were made by village craftsmen, combining the trades of wheelwright and wagon-builder with those of carpenter and joiner.

Harvest wagons of the eighteenth century were greatly influenced by the design of carrier's wagons but acquired local characteristics, depending on topography and the nature of the soil. In some areas of clay and heavy soil a broad-wheeled wagon was used, while on lighter soil, such as chalk, farm vehicles had lighter frames and narrower tyres. The main distinctions lay between the heavier **box wagon** of the flat eastern counties of England and the lighter, shallower **bow wagon** of the undulating western regions. It is interesting to note that during the eighteenth and nineteenth centuries wagons were almost unknown in the North of England (apart from north Humberside), the highlands of Wales and the moorland regions of Devon and Cornwall. Those wagons used in Scotland were mainly introduced by English families.

During the second half of the nineteenth century there was a decline in local craftsmanship due to competition from larger firms, based on industrial towns, with up-to-date methods of production. Later farm wagons were of simple design with plank sides and iron naves or hubs, known as **barge wagons.** This type, unlike the older wagons with waisted sides for half and quarter lock, often had full underlock. During the last decade of the Victorian era there was a slightly smaller and shallower type, with outward sloping sides and full underlock, known as a **boat wagon.** Some boat wagons had semi-elliptical leaf springs in the style of a modern carriage. By the 1900s the older panel-sided farm wagon of tradition, solid and unsprung, was becoming a thing of the past. Even the village craftsman was beginning to imitate factory designs, traditional methods being killed off not only by the coming of the motor vehicle but also by the progress of industry and mass-production.

Another late vehicle used on farms, from the 1890s, was the **trolley** or open dray, popular in western Yorkshire and the West Midlands until the period of the Second World War. A version of the trolley was also used by coal merchants and the cartage departments of the railway companies.

### The Kentish hop wagon

This was a specialised agricultural vehicle, on four wheels, used mainly in the hop gardens of south-east England. It had large rear wheels and smaller front wheels, with tyres at least eight inches wide, although strakes were frequently used until the 1900s. There were high, almost vertical ladders or supports at front and rear, although the sides were not always fully boarded in, especially at the front end. The hop wagon would be used, in season, to carry both hop poles and bales of hops.

## Carts

Two-wheeled carts have always been more widely used than wagons in highland districts. They were more economical on small farms and for short hauls, requiring one horse in place of a larger team, although for heavier loads a second horse could be used in tandem, as a chain horse, or with extra side gear known as an outrigger. This latter was more widely used in military circles than on farms.

The traditional two-wheeled (sometimes two-horsed) cart developed from the wain of the sixteenth and seventeenth centuries. A similar type of vehicle was used in Wales and Cornwall until the end of the nineteenth century. There was also a popular version associated with the Cotswolds and south Midlands. The wain was about ten feet long and slightly over six feet wide, being a mere platform for the load, with protection over the wheels and raised ladders or front and rear boards. Some later versions had low panel or spindle sides, while in parts of Wales there were primitive vehicles with basket or wickerwork sides.

The great advantages of the two-wheeled vehicle were its comparative ease of manoeuvre and also the way in which it might be adapted for tipping, as in carting manure and building materials. Early carts, drawn by a single horse, were frequently known as **dung carts** and used almost exclusively for spreading manure over the land. A notable feature of the dung cart was its lengthwise rather than cross boarding of the floor, which made it easier to scrape out with fork or rake. Most wooden structures tend to warp, and smaller cross planks formed awkward ridges, adding to the difficulty of scraping out. The average two-wheeled cart, sometimes known as a tumbril, carried a load of between

*Fig. 8. Wain.*

*Fig. 9. Hermaphrodite.*

twenty and twenty-two hundredweights.

Plank-sided or **scotch carts** were widely used in eastern England from the mid nineteenth century, this type being introduced by Scottish farmers who bought large areas of land from bankrupt East Anglian yeomen at a time of agricultural depression. Scotch carts were mostly factory-made and strictly utilitarian, although a few were later constructed by local craftsmen.

### The hermaphrodite

A composite vehicle or hermaphrodite appears to have been a cross between a cart and a wagon. It was really a two-wheeled cart with an extra pair of wheels, attached as a forecarriage, the latter supporting an extended ladder or horizontal platform. They could be bought for about £20 each, which was less than half the price of a four-wheeled harvest wagon. The fore part was easy to detach, so that the rear or hind part could be used as an ordinary cart.

### Vehicles for the carriage of timber

Other notable vehicles, seen mainly in the country, would be used to convey lengths of timber, either wood for building purposes or whole logs taken from forest to sawmill. The earliest of these was the **timber bob,** known in some parts of the country as a **neb.** They consisted mainly of a large pair of wheels on an arched axle, the log or length of wood being suspended from the underside by chains. There were large, small and medium bobs, the largest on record having wheels eight feet in diameter. Later bobs were fitted with a windlass device on the shafts for raising the load clear of the ground or moving it into position.

Four-wheeled **timber carriages** or **tugs** were also used, having both iron and wooden axles. Rear wheels were usually slightly larger than front wheels, although smaller types tended to be equirotal. Bolsters on fore and hind carriages had both chains and stanchions to keep the load in place.

## The miller's wagon or cart

This was a vehicle frequently seen in both town and country. It was panel-sided and resembled a harvest wagon, but with a higher loading platform than most agricultural types. Sacks of grain and flour were usually loaded or unloaded on to high platforms or through upper-storey apertures by means of block and tackle.

## Early town vehicles

Vehicles used in towns, apart from those for private or public passenger transport, were of limited range until the second half of the nineteenth century. The main exceptions would be drays, carts and wagons used by brewers, the panel-sided wagons used by millers, water-barrel wagons or carts, and vehicles for distributing coal. Chimney-sweeps would have two-wheeled open-ended carts for their rods and brushes, drawn by a pony or donkey, while at one time the open-ended dead-horse cart of the knacker would be fairly commonplace. Builders, general merchants and warehouse or factory owners would have carts and wagons not dissimilar to those used by the farmer, although often having full underlock. The latter was necessary on all four-wheeled vehicles for turning in narrow streets and yards.

While many farm wagons and agricultural vehicles have been preserved in museums of rural life, transport museums and private collections, very few of the older town vehicles survive. Information concerning them may, however, be gleaned from the work of contemporary artists, especially the sketches of such topographical draughtsmen as Paul and Thomas Sandby, renowned for their views of Windsor during the mid eighteenth century, many of which show street scenes of the period from 1740 to 1770. Among finished watercolours by Paul Sandby is a view of 'The Store Tower, Windsor Castle, from Castle Hill', with a water cart or wagon in the foreground. This vehicle is a large barrel mounted horizontally on four wheels, the framework of the undercarriage forming a still of massive beams. A single horse

*Fig. 10. Water-barrel cart, early nineteenth century.*

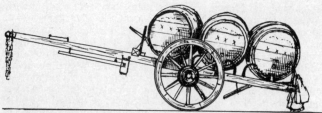

*Fig. 11. Two-wheeled brewer's dray, eighteenth century.*

between shafts is ridden by a nondescript youth in ragged clothing. There is also an interesting two-wheeled brewer's dray, drawn by two horses, in a watercolour of 'Henry VIII's Gateway from Castle Hill', and a similar vehicle appears in a view of 'Windsor Castle from Isherwood's Brewery in Datchet Lane'. The design of the drays is akin to that of the traditional cart or wain of the period, as used in Wales and Cornwall, but without end ladders and protection for the wheels. The firm of Samuel Whitbread keeps such a vehicle for publicity purposes; it appears at horse and agricultural shows, with the driver and attendants wearing eighteenth-century costume. This type usually carried three large barrels mounted in a crosswise position, the driver frequently riding on the first barrel, or upwards of a dozen smaller barrels. With a heavy load, requiring chain horses, the driver's mate or trouncer would be in charge of the lead horse.

An even more interesting study in pencil and wash shows a wagon belonging to Sir William Watkins Wynn. This is a simple carrying box on four large wheels, although the rear wheels are much larger than those at the front. The panel-sided body is raised well clear of the road and has suspension in the form of elbow springs (iron columns and leather straps). There is a high box-seat for the driver but no evidence of brakes. The purpose of this vehicle, dated at 1772, is somewhat obscure; the picture appears to have been part of a set of Welsh views made near the English border. The wagon has all the indications of a vehicle drawn by two horses, obviously made for speed, and may have been used to collect game after shooting or stag hunting. In some ways it resembles a fourgon or continental luggage wagon, perhaps used for small, precious items, although in this case the loading platform would be inconveniently high. These studies and watercolours form part of the Royal Collection at Windsor.

**Coal carts**

The coal cart or wagon, of a type popular in London until the mid 1950s, may be occasionally glimpsed in the paintings and sketches of the French artist Gericault, who spent some time in England during the 1820s. This was a spindle-sided, bow-fronted vehicle with a solid tailboard and a shelf for scales and weights between the rear wheels. It had a high loading platform, large wheels and a short wheelbase. The sides curved to a high, rounded frontboard displaying the name and address of the coal merchant. This vehicle first appeared during the eighteenth century and, although it remained popular in London for over 150 years it was not widely used in the provinces, where it was ousted by a flat trolley without raised sides but frequently having a centre bar or partition. Coal wagons, especially the London type, were drawn by a single horse and usually operated in pairs. On encountering a steep gradient one vehicle would be left at the foot of the incline while its horse was hitched in tandem to the other vehicle, acting as a chain horse until reaching the summit. Both horses would then return for the vehicle left at the foot of the hill and repeat the process.

Much larger vehicles, usually plank-sided and drawn by three or more horses, were needed to bring coal in bulk from the wharf to the merchant's yard.

*Fig. 12. London-type coal cart, late eighteenth century onwards.*

*Fig. 13. London builder's cart.*

**Builder's carts**

Builders made frequent use of horse-drawn vehicles until the 1940s, especially two-wheeled tip carts in various sizes. Similar types were also used in quarries, brickworks and by general contractors, there being a smaller size for a cob or small draught horse and a much larger vehicle for the Shire type, representing larger breeds. Such vehicles were advertised in the *Clay Worker*, the magazine of the brick and tile industry, until shortly after the Second World War.

The standard one-horse builder's cart, with sideboards or raves above wheel level and the upper front projecting straight (flat) to carry an extra load, could hold up to six hundred bricks and cost between £16 and £26 from the works. The London-pattern builder's cart was of even sturdier construction, being panel-sided and projecting slightly further at the front than the standard type. Sideboards above the wheels were often detachable.

Dressed stone or marble was frequently brought to a building site in a low-slung, panel-sided cart, with straight shafts, drawn by

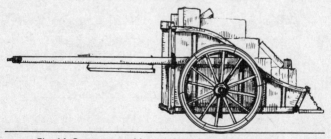

*Fig. 14. Stone or marble cart, late eighteenth century.*

two or more horses in tandem. This had large wheels and cranked axles, resembling a larger and clumsier version of the two-wheeled float. As with the London coal wagon the sides rose to a high frontboard through graceful curves.

## The general-purpose float

A vehicle widely used during the second half of the nineteenth century was the cranked-axle cart or general-purpose float, of which the stone and marble cart was a precursor rather than an enlarged version. It appeared in three main sizes, all being low-slung with cranked axles and two large wheels. Some of these vehicles had extensive side rails or sideboards for overhanging loads. The low platforms were ideal for loading kegs, barrels and churns at street level. The light or cob-sized cart, at about £25, was

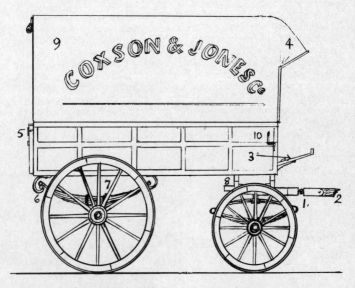

*Fig. 15. Typical medium-heavy van: 1 elliptical springs, 2 shafts, 3 footboard, 4 canopy, 5 tailboard, 6 scroll iron, 7 semi-elliptical springs, 8 futchels, 9 head or cover, 10 lamp bracket.*

an ideal milk-delivery float, and would carry up to fifteen hundredweight. The medium or light draught-horse size carried up to one ton, costing an extra £5, while the heavy draught-horse size took up to a ton and a half and cost between £30 and £35, according to finish.

## Other general-purpose vehicles

General-purpose vehicles of the nineteenth century, remaining popular for well over seventy years, were four-wheeled wagons with either flat or bow fronts and full underlock, able to carry between four and six tons and costing between £45 and £70. These were strongly made, yet comparatively light and compact, with outer raves or sideboards to support an overhanging load. They were considered ideal for brewers and could be fitted with hoops and waterproof covers. The driver sat on a box-seat above and in front of the carrying body. This was a sprung vehicle with semi-elliptical leaf springs above fore and hind wheels, drawn by one or more horses, according to the load. A good medium draught horse could handle up to two tons.   Lighter deliveries could be made by tradesmen in much smaller, lower vehicles, also fully sprung, costing between £28 and £35. Such wagons or vans were recommended for wine merchants, dairymen and for the conveyance of all light goods. They could be used, as with the larger general-purpose vehicle, either open or covered, but usually the former. This type would be driven to a light horse or cob. Those with hand-lever or foot-pedal brakes were slightly more expensive than the ordinary type.

Not all vehicles were fitted with brakes, although these became more widely used towards the end of the nineteenth century. Some larger wagons had hand-wound screw-down brakes, although the

*Fig. 16. Light trade van, 1870.*

hand or foot brake applying a metal or wooden block to the rear wheels was more frequently seen on lighter and medium wagons likely to travel at speed. There was no effective braking for two-wheeled carts. A drag shoe was fitted under a rear wheel of most wagons, usually on the near side, to prevent it overrunning the team when going down hill. What was known as a roller scotch or scotch roller, connected to hub or bodywork by chains, fitted behind a rear wheel to prevent a vehicle running backwards on a slope.

Vehicles working after dark used side lamps, usually candles, but later oil lamps. These were known as van lamps as opposed to carriage and coach lamps, but could be of any serviceable type. Vehicles used by the General Post Office had lamps similar to those on the original mail-coaches.

# 3. Delivery vehicles

It was not until the second half of the nineteenth century that trade delivery vehicles began to acquire greater range and variety. This related to the increased wealth and prosperity of Great Britain during the period from the 1860s to the Edwardian era. Trade flourished and with it the need to advertise and render a better service than other firms in the same line of business. The butcher, baker or dairyman with a smart turnout was more likely to be patronised by wealthier customers, while even the humblest street trader invested in the best he could afford.

**Bakery vehicles**

Bakers began with two-wheeled carts, not unlike gigs, usually drawn by a pony or cob. These had a high rail behind the driver's seat, enclosing the flat top of the carrying box, where baskets could be placed. Access to the inner compartment was through double doors at the rear. During the 1890s a four-wheeled van made its appearance, remaining popular with some firms and individual traders until the second half of the twentieth century. Most bakery vans were fairly light, with full underlock, and drawn by a large cob or by a vanner — a medium-weight draught horse between a cob and a heavy carthorse. Early four-wheeled vans tended to be flat-roofed rather than round-topped, while later vehicles had slightly curved roofs, sloping forward or downwards at the front end. Most had a double driving seat above the forecarriage, with an ample dashboard, although this was sometimes reduced to a low rail.

Bread vans were of various sizes but mostly had a short wheelbase and shafts with an upward curve. Some two-wheelers, especially early models, were panel-sided, while the four-wheelers were more likely to have arched hoops and canvas tops with front

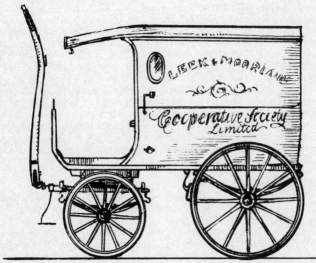

Fig. 17. Bread van.

and rear flaps. The more enclosed type of driving seat, almost a cab, often had side windows. Some later vehicles had sliding doors at the side of the bodywork for access to the interior.

**Butchery vehicles**

High-class butchers greatly prided themselves on swift and efficient delivery services. Their delivery boys, in white jackets and horizontally striped blue aprons, drove pony-sized vehicles similar

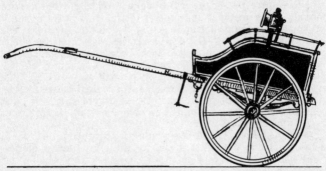

Fig. 18. Butcher's cart.

21

to small gigs, with straight sides and no dashboard. The driving seat was reached by iron steps from the slightly curved shafts, with one step (step-iron) on either side of the vehicle. There were usually prominent side lamps and an iron or brass rail round the top of the bodywork, as with the early baker's cart. Similar, but perhaps less showy, vehicles were also kept by fishmongers and to collect newspapers at the main-line stations.

During the 1920s and 1930s there were a number of vehicles used not only by individual butchers but also by the butchery and cooked-meat departments of large stores and co-operative societies that traded in outlying suburbs. These were almost shops on wheels, with built-in refrigerators, a serving counter under a side or rear awning, and large display windows. Most of them were equirotal and mounted on pneumatic tyres.

## Milk-delivery vehicles

Milk deliveries were, for many years, made with three-wheeled handcarts or barrows, seen in the West End of London until the late 1930s. The low-slung float on cranked axles, first used by farmers as a general-purpose or market cart, was not widely seen until the late 1890s. This proved ideal for the large churns of the day, which could be loaded through a rear door on to the low platform without much difficulty.

In later years, when bottled milk was first introduced, the larger dairy companies used fleets of four-wheeled carts or wagons, light and well sprung. Some, driven from a box-seat, were of a square or oblong shape, with full underlock, and known as **box carts.** There were sliding panels on either side for access to the interior, while further crates were stacked on the slatted roof — mainly empties. Other milk-delivery vehicles were known as the 'step-in' type; some had the front almost completely enclosed by a windscreen and were entered like a cab by means of a low step. The enclosed type had apertures for the reins, but such vehicles, while easy to mount, were sometimes dangerous to drive, there being a chance of the horse gaining control by getting its tail over the reins. The centre of gravity, with the step-in vehicle, was very low, which made it heavier than it should have been and something of a horse-killer. In the Midlands and North of England a familiar type of vehicle was a covered trolley or small dray with an open front, but protected by a solid rear panel or raised tailboard. The sides were open but protected by weatherproof curtains. Each vehicle of this type was mounted on semi-elliptical leaf springs at both front and back.

After the Second World War a number of rather curious milk-delivery vehicles were constructed for use by the larger dairies. Most had bodywork of light metal alloys and very small front wheels, about ten inches in diameter and close together.

*Fig. 19. Milk-delivery box-van.*

Dairy carts and floats of all types were among the first horse-drawn commercial vehicles to be fitted with pneumatic tyres — about 1933. This was to decrease the noise of early morning deliveries in large towns and seaside resorts, where late risers dreaded to be awakened at the crack of dawn. At one time there were special four-wheeled delivery vans for sterilised milk, not unlike bread vans. When all types of bottled milk began to be delivered by the same roundsmen, most of the special vehicles were switched to the bakery departments. Milk and bread vans had screw-down brakes, mainly to stop the horse or pony wandering away if left to its own devices. A good horse, however, often a Welsh cob or crossbred of this type, would soon learn the round, knowing exactly when to stop and when to move.

### Greengrocery vehicles

Fresh vegetables, fruit and cut flowers were sold in London streets from long barrows of a type that could be pushed by hand or drawn by a pony. Some street traders, however, preferred a flat trolley or pony dray. The latter types were more frequently seen in northern England.

The co-operative societies showed great initiative in this sphere during the 1920s and 1930s, using a wide range of covered vehicles for fruit, vegetables and sometimes wet fish. The main type was open at the sides, with items displayed in neat trays, partitioned down the centre. Both ends of the vehicle had solid panels, while there were lockers and containers for the heavier root vegetables

23

between the rear wheels, and also a locker with a hinged lid on the rear part of the roof. There were iron steps at the centre-side for access to the roof, usually with two rungs. The driver's seat above the frontboard was roofed over by a canopy and reached by a step-iron from the shafts. A rack or shelf ran down the centre of the vehicle, while the sides were opened in four sections, two each side, protected by roller-type shutters drawn from above. The vehicle was well sprung and of modern design with pneumatic tyres and van-type mudguards, the wheels having polished brass or chromium hub-caps.

An earlier type of greengrocery cart or dray, appearing mainly in the Greater London area, although rarely seen after the Second World War, was sometimes known as the **hawker's cart** and could be used for any type of merchandise from firewood to hardware. The wheels were fairly small, especially at the front end, with a low platform and comparatively long wheelbase. The lower part was similar to a totter's vehicle, still widely used by the totter or scrap-merchant, although the hawker's cart was frequently covered or headed, its sides and rear protected by roller-blinds let down from eye level. There might even have been a flat or rounded canvas top on hoops, the space between it and the original roof fitted with extra shelves and storage space, giving it a somewhat top-heavy appearance. The street trader using this type of vehicle was often a

*Fig. 20. Old-type laundry van.*

hawker in the original sense of the word, not so much with regular calls but touting for custom at the top of his voice.

## Grocery vans

Grocery vans, for the delivery of dry goods and branded items sold in tins, bottles and jars, might be low, square-shaped vehicles on either two or four wheels. The most popular version, however, was a two-wheeled covered van, similar to a large type of gig known as a Manchester market cart. It had large wheels, straight shafts, panelled sides and a fairly low frontboard, without footboard and dashboard. Mounted by a step-iron on the shaft, the driving seat was a mere cross plank. Further back the interior, under a canvas cover on hoops, had shelves, racks and compartments. Many items such as flour, tea and coffee were measured out to the householder from large containers rather than sold already wrapped. All tradesmen had to carry a full set of weights and scales on their delivery vehicles, by law.

Some larger vans and wagons owned by grocers were kept for the collection of bulk consignments at railway stations and markets, while others might be used to deliver large orders to hotels and boarding houses.

## Laundry vans

These were of two main types, one slightly larger than the other. Both were four-wheeled vehicles, well sprung with full underlock. The more popular type, widely seen throughout the provinces, resembled a large bread van in outward appearance; it had rear doors and was stacked inside with hamper-like laundry baskets. Some vans, however, had access from the front only, while others had tailboards letting down through 180 degrees, with two flap doors (half-doors) above.

An earlier, more traditional type of van, surviving until the mid 1950s, mainly in London and the neighbouring counties, had a high, square body with flat rather than panelled sides, covered by a canvas top on hoops. There was also a high-perched driving seat, the entire width of the low footboard, seldom having a proper dashboard.

While drivers of vans owned by bakers, butchers, greengrocers and fishmongers usually wore long aprons and sometimes straw hats, laundrymen wore long white coats and peaked caps.

## Coal wagons

Coal-delivery vehicles changed very little from the late eighteenth to the mid twentieth centuries, although there were fewer of the spindle-sided or London types to be seen after the First World War. There were, however, several regional variations, although the London type occasionally appeared in the larger cities of the Midlands and North of England. The most enduring vehicle was the flat trolley, usually having a centre partition, especially in southern and south-eastern England. A rounded or shield-shaped board at the side of the vehicle, midway between back and front wheels, was used by the coalman for chalking up the latest prices. Wheels on the trolley-type vehicle were fairly small in proportion and frequently equirotal. The headboard was often quite large and brightly painted with the name of the owner, usually supported above a row of straight bars or spindles. Some trolleys in the North of England had a fixed tailboard only, while special trolleys in the Manchester area, used mainly for smaller bags of coal, were entirely flat without partitions, headboards or tailboards. Some coal-delivery vehicles were fitted with a single driver's seat, supported by straight or curved irons, although many were driven from a standing position behind the frontboard or led through the streets.

## Vehicles used by tailors, hatters, etc.

Some fashionable tailors, hatters and haberdashers ran delivery services for their favoured customers. These could have been either two-wheeled or four-wheeled vehicles, seldom custom-built and frequently hybrids adapted from other vehicles. Many of these, however, appeared both smart and elegant, especially when drawn by a high-stepping hackney in the care of a liveried coachman and groom. Scotts, the hatters of Old Bond Street, Piccadilly, had a picturesque brougham-like vehicle in shiny black with yellow wheels and gold, red-shaded lettering. Rothmans, the tobacconists, also of Piccadilly, still use a similar type of vehicle, although slightly larger and driven to a pair of greys rather than to a single horse. The brougham-type used by Scotts was hired to

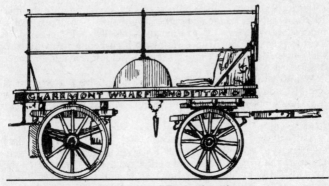

Fig. 21. South of England coal cart.

*Fig. 22. Hatter's delivery vehicle.*

them by a firm of jobbers specialising in this type of work. Many concerns, however, kept their own stables, including a Worcester firm of tailors and haberdashers that formerly ran two vehicles during the period after the Second World War, one a brougham-type and the other a two-wheeled cart converted from a butcher's delivery vehicle. These were in daily use until the early 1960s, although the larger type, perhaps less handy in traffic, was eventually loaned for display to the Hereford and Worcester County Museum at Hartlebury Castle, near Kidderminster.

## Vehicles used by brewers and vintners

Like coal-delivery vehicles, the wagons and drays used by brewers were also modelled on traditional lines. Although the two-wheeled dray has almost disappeared, the four-wheeled dray with high sides, either covered or open, is still in use for short hauls and also as a show wagon for publicity purposes. They often appear in trade classes at the larger agricultural and horse shows, serving as useful advertisements before large audiences. Several other concerns have recently taken advantage of this kind of publicity.

Variations of the standard brewer's dray are found mainly in comparative sizes and lengths of wheelbase. The older types, in use until the period between the world wars, were often much longer than modern versions. Lighter wagons and vans were used for delivering crates of bottled beer, wines and spirits, drawn either by a single horse or a pair of horses. The traditional driving position for the brewer's drayman was fairly high, on raised irons, at the centre front. The assistant or trouncer stood just behind the driver on his left-hand side.

*Fig. 23. Furniture van, 1901.*

**Furniture vans**

Horse-drawn furniture vans were a familiar sight at one period, a few surviving until the late 1930s. From the 1900s some were drawn in road trains of three or more vehicles by a small traction engine. A small version could be pulled by a single horse in shafts, but most used a pair of heavy horses harnessed on either side of a centre pole. Both large and small vans had slightly arched roofs, with a space on top for extra furniture, protected by rounding boards. The floor of the van, in the rear half, was in the form of a well. The bodywork had ledge sides overhanging the wheels, but conforming to the radius of the larger rear wheels. The driving seat was on or near the roof, while there were flap doors (half-doors) at the back, with a tailboard large enough to let down as a ramp. There was very low clearance above ground level. Rear wheels were cranked.

The whole vehicle was usually painted with bold, ornate lettering in bright colours, advertising that households could be removed, safes hoisted and offices filled. The museum at St Albans has a large, oblong furniture van of the 1900s, mounted on small equirotal wheels, but this appears to be an exceptional type.

From the 1900s some furniture could be sent by sea, road or rail in large containers mounted on flat trolleys designed for the purpose. The container was lifted on to the trolley or railway wagon by crane power. Most furniture vans, however, were trundled by their horses to the nearest station yard and run on to a carriage truck from a loading bay or bank. They would then make a journey by fast goods train to the town of destination, to be collected by agents with a hired team.

**Ice and ice-cream vehicles**

Ice carts were occasionally seen in large cities until the 1900s. The London version, a similar type also appearing in the provinces, would be panel-sided, mounted on two wheels and

28

usually painted in florid colours and letters with the name of an Italian owner. A larger box-like wagon on four wheels, often drawn by a pair of horses, was less frequently seen in dockland areas, especially on the east coast. It may be noted that much of the ice was imported by Norwegian vessels from across the North Sea.

Ice-cream carts were usually pulled by a small pony, led rather than driven. The typical cart, sometimes known as a barrow, had two small wheels on cranked axles. The canopy or awning, to protect it from the summer sun, was usually striped with a deep valance at the sides, the whole supported on twisted brass rods. There was an abundance of highly polished metalwork, for both handrails and the lids covering the containers. Lettering, either on the awning or the sides of the vehicle, was highly colourful and smacked of the fairground. A firm operating in South Yorkshire once had a number of identical vehicles, each bearing the remarkable slogan: 'Patronised by the clergy, nobility and gentry'.

### Railway cartage

Most railway-owned vehicles, apart from a few earmarked for internal work at large depots, belonged to the cartage or delivery service. They were as varied as the consignments of merchandise normally sent by rail, including light and heavy parcels vans, timber carriages, drays, wagons, trolleys and even special low-loaders for boilers and heavy machinery.

Most of these vehicles were used by the main-line companies until nationalisation, while a number were retained by British Railways and could still be seen in station yards until the early 1960s. As late as 1928 there were 32,171 carts and vans in daily service, against a total of 2,837 motor vehicles. These figures do not include the smaller independent, joint and subsidiary companies, such as the Metropolitan Railway and the Midland and Great Northern Joint Committee lines, all of which had a number of horse-drawn vans and drays.

The most familiar vehicle was the **single-horse wagon,** sometimes driven to a pair, in which case the shafts were replaced by a centre pole. This type would be slightly less than a ton in tare weight, with a capacity of two tons. The officially recognised load limit in London was thirty-five hundredweights for a single horse and three tons ten hundredweights for a pair, the latter naturally applying to even larger vehicles than the above. The single-horse wagon had full underlock and was mounted on semi-elliptical leaf springs. There was a high box-seat mounted on straight or curved irons, with a footboard at forty-five degrees and a hand-lever brake operating on the rear wheels, while the sides would be of planks supported by strong ironwork. Raves or sideboards would protect the wheels and help to support an overhanging load. On many types there were alternate planks and iron bars, bars fitting horizontally between the planks. Each vehicle carried a drag shoe, hung in chains on the near side, midway between back and front wheels. There was also a small range of heavier wagons drawn by teams of quality Shire horses known as 'waggoners', often the pride of the stud.

Most companies owned a variety of **single-horse vans,** the most popular being the passenger-train parcel van of the express delivery service, the roof of which might be boarded up inside and covered on the outside with canvas or tarpaulin. The flat top curved downwards at the sides to an overhanging ledge about a foot above the rear wheels. As with the single-horse wagon there would be leaf springs and full underlock. Parcel vans were often panel-sided, eliminating apertures between panels and planks. The average van of this type would be fourteen hundredweights tare weight, although some were much lighter and smaller at seven hundredweights three quarters. A few had barred windows on either side of the driving seat, which was in a central position with a small, square footboard at an angle of sixty degrees. A tailboard, slightly lower than the sideboards, would let down from the back and was frequently chained at an angle of thirty degrees to support an overhanging load. The upper part of the rear entrance would be protected by a roll of tarpaulin secured by straps. A van boy accompanied each driver to assist with loading and unloading; he would be sent by cab to the nearest company stables, in case of

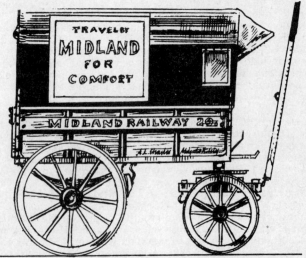

*Fig. 24. Parcels-delivery van, Midland Railway Company, 1914.*

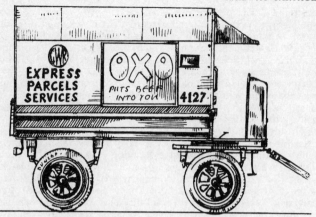

*Fig. 25. Modern railway delivery van.*

an accident, to fetch a spare horse. He would frequently stand at the back of the van, hanging on to a cord from the roof.

Much smaller, lighter vehicles in railway service included open **spring-carts,** some used for departmental duties and not unlike a sprung version of the scotch cart. There was also a range of single-horse, two-wheeled parcel vans. Many of the latter, especially those used by the Great Western, Midland and Great Northern Railways, were as light and elegant as carriages.

In some areas, especially the manufacturing towns of central England, the **single-horse trolley,** also known as a lorry, trulley or rulley, was a familiar sight from the 1890s. This was a flat, dray-like vehicle in both sprung and unsprung versions, sometimes having screw-down brakes, but usually without a driver's seat. The single horse was usually led through the streets but was sometimes driven from a standing position on the front of the platform.

The average trolley was seventeen hundredweight tare weight, with a capacity of two tons. Chain horses were frequently used on steep inclines and with the maximum load. Most later vehicles were equirotal and also had detachable shafts to be interchanged with a drawbar for mechanical (tractor) haulage. After the Second World War a number were constructed without springs but mounted on pneumatic tyres.

A number of parcels delivery vans survived nationalisation, while drays and trolleys were seen in fair numbers until the late 1950s. The ultimate expression of design in this sphere was a **single-horse van** of a type first used by the Great Western Railway at Oxford station and later copied by the other main-line companies. The prototype entered service in October 1937 and similar types were used, in all parts of Britain, for at least twenty years. Among other features, it had motorcar-type wheels on pneumatic tyres, ball bearings, hub brakes and electric headlamps (battery). A scuttlebox dashboard resembled the bonnet of a motor van, so that many laymen wrongly though that such vehicles had been reconstructed from old motor vans. The van also had a long wheelbase and equirotal wheels of small diameter. Whatever its merits or defects, it certainly had the modern image and was widely appreciated on that account.

The high-capacity low-loading vehicle mentioned above, mainly used for boilers and castings, was known as a **boiler trolley**. A typical example was produced at Swindon works about 1905, and also by several other companies with main lines through industrial areas. It consisted of a low undercarriage of lateral steel girders, with crosswise bolsters at either end, above fore and hind carriages. Wheels were of the solid disc type, of steel throughout, on broad steel tyres. They were slightly larger at the back than the front with full underlock on the forecarriage. Draught gear was in the form of double shafts. Tare weight was six tons four hundredweights and capacity forty tons.

Prize cattle and other livestock were frequently conveyed to and from showground or market in low-slung open vehicles, with panel sides and either two or four wheels. The four-wheeled type had cranked rear wheels.

A number of horse-drawn railway vehicles of the cartage service, during the first half of the twentieth century, had what were known as artillery wheels. These resembled the wheels of guns and military wagons of the First World War, having iron naves with dust excluders, and additional spokes for extra strength and longer wear. There were several types of genuine artillery wheel but the railway versions (large and small) were only roughly similar to any of them.

# 4. Public utility and special vehicles

Almost everything portable and mounted on wheels appeared as some form of horse-drawn vehicle. The more obvious examples included a wide range in public service, from fire-engines and ambulances to various types of cart and wagon used in street cleaning and refuse collection. In the days of street trams there were even fully horsed service departments to maintain overhead wires and standards, these having four-wheeled trucks with folding or telescopic ladders. Road-making and repair departments had horse-drawn tar-boilers mounted on four small iron wheels from 1908, when tar-spraying was introduced.

1. Nineteenth-century timber bob, or neb, at St Albans City Museum.

2. A London coal cart.

3. A heavy delivery wagon, as used by haulage contractors from the 1860s to the present day.

4. Birmingham Co-operative Society Bakery Department van no. 60 photographed in a Birmingham street, 1951.

5. Van 88, of the same type as that in plate 4, at a steam rally at Marsh Gibbon, Bucks, in 1973.

6. Old-type bread van, with added superstructure, originally built for Edmonton Co-operative Society about 1910, seen here in Ilford, 1949.

7. *Early twentieth-century bread van, now at Leicester Transport Museum.*

8. *On its rounds c. 1922, an old-type bread van, with added superstructure, belonging to Filby Bros of Manor Park, London.*

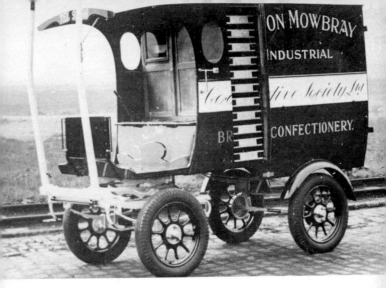

9. A modern (1938) bakery van on pneumatic tyres. It was built at the CWS van works, Manchester.

10. A typical butcher's cart of the London area, c. 1901.

11. The first design of mobile butcher's shop, built by CWS and shown at the Edinburgh Congress Exhibition, 1923.

12. Early box-type milk-delivery van, belonging to Handsworth Dairies Ltd, Birmingham, 1951.

13. Modern 'step-in' type milk van (1938), used by Slough and District Co-operative Society and built at the CWS van works.

14. A box-type milk-delivery van, 1962.

15. Late 1950s milk-delivery van, built by A. Creasey of South Norwood for the Midland Counties Dairy, Birmingham.

16. London-type hawker's van used for greengrocery, owned by Walduck Bros of Forest Gate and photographed in 1949.

17. Milk-delivery van of a type used in the North of England, built at the CWS van works, Manchester, c. 1928.

18. Greengrocery van, also used for selling fish, game and poultry, and built by the CWS van works.

19. A two-wheeled grocer's delivery van at Epping in 1902, decorated in honour of the coronation of Edward VII.

20. Two oxen harnessed to a van built by Connelly's of Hereford for Hugon's, suet manufacturers of Manchester, c. 1920.

21. A line-up of Birmingham Co-operative Society box-type laundry vans, c. 1936.

22. Large modern van on pneumatic tyres, used to supply hotels and restaurants with greengroceries.

23. A standard-type coal cart or trolley, c. 1960.

24. Two-wheeled brewery dray of eighteenth-century type, used by Whitbread's.

25. A brewer's dray of the old type, with long wheelbase, c. 1900.

26. In Sandwich, Kent, c. 1900, a brewer's turnout for bottled beer in crates.

27. Open wagon used by the Great Western Railway for general cartage purposes, built at Swindon, 1905.

28. Furniture van, c. 1900. A type normally drawn by horses but here towed by a steam traction engine.

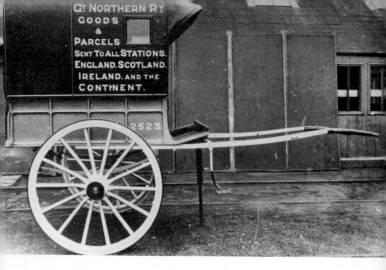

29. *Two-wheeled parcels delivery van. Great Northern Railway, just completed at Doncaster Works, c. 1912.*

30. *Hearse for a single horse between shafts, c. 1900.*

31. Horse-drawn fire-engine (steam pump), c. 1890, at Leicester Transport Museum.

32. Two-roomed saloon-type showman's living van, built by Savage Bros of King's Lynn c. 1900.

**Fire-engines**

During the Victorian era the fire department had the greatest romantic appeal for the layman, as a horse-drawn fire-engine tearing through the streets, often belching sparks and tongues of flame, was enough to raise a cheer from any bystanders.

Until the mid eighteenth century most fire-fighting appliances were hand-drawn trolleys, the manual pumps worked by side levers. Later hand-manual pumps, however, were horse-drawn, as was the first engine with a steam fire pump, jointly invented by Braithwaite and Ericsson in 1829.

Many early fire-engines were privately owned, especially those used on large estates, often depending for their water supply on ornamental lakes. One of these, formerly used at Dodington Park near Old Sodbury, Avon, was typical of the small hand-built machines of the mid eighteenth century. It was pulled by a single horse between shafts and mounted on four small wheels of the heavy cart type, with full underlock. The parallel pump handles on either side of the vehicle could be operated by six people, three aside, anyone available from the domestic staff or estate workers being pressed into service. This particular engine was made for Dodington House by Hadley Simpkin of Long Acre, London, a part of the city renowned for the construction of stagecoaches and other horse-drawn vehicles.

In larger towns fire-fighting was the concern of insurance companies, each company having a brigade dressed in its own colourful uniforms. An aquatint by James Pollard, published in 1825, shows the appliances of three companies and a manually drawn parish pump rushing to the scene of an extensive fire. While the engines of the Westminster Company and the County Fire Company are drawn by pairs of spirited coach-horses driven from the box, the Phoenix engine is of a novel two-wheeled design drawn by carthorses in tandem and guided by men running alongside. Men riding on the engines hold lighted torches to guide them through the badly lit streets of the period, none of the vehicles seeming to have either candle or oil lamps. It may be noted that the steam fire-engine of Braithwaite and Ericsson, although used experimentally for a number of years, in competition with hand-manual engines, was first adopted for public service in the United States of America. Steam fire-engines were not widely used in Britain until the 1860s. The establishment of a fully trained Metropolitan Brigade, independent of private enterprises, dated from the Fire Brigade Act of 1865.

The Ericsson engine was designed on a four-wheeled carriage, reinforced with heavy ironwork, to be drawn by two horses, the whole mounted on leaf springs and having full underlock. A vertical boiler was mounted between the rear wheels. Waste gases escaped through a pipe (designed to resemble the head of a

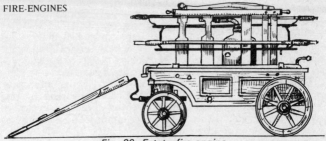

*Fig. 26. Estate fire-engine.*

dragon) directly behind the box, but pointing backwards and away from the driver. A further novelty was its iron rather than wooden spoked wheels, the spokes being rods of cast iron, designed well in advance of the period.

Later fire-engines, as used until the period of the First World War, although gradually replaced by mechanically propelled vehicles from 1899, were mainly of wooden construction, apart from the boiler and pumps. The most popular of these was the 'double vertical' or 'London vertical' type, invented by James Shand and introduced during the 1880s by the firm of Shand Mason. This was also known as the '350-gallon engine', having double-acting steam cylinders capable of pumping that amount of water per minute. Hand-lever brakes acted on the rear wheels, while the undercarriage was mounted on semi-elliptical leaf springs. The captain or officer-in-charge shared a raised box-seat with the driver, while the other firemen sat back to back, near the centre of the engine, on lengthwise seating. A specially trained fireman-engineer manned the boiler and pumps from a low rear

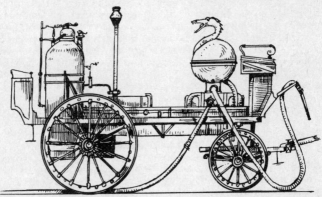

*Fig. 27. The first horse-drawn steam fire-engine.*

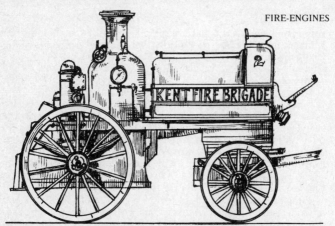

*Fig. 28. Steam fire engine, 1890s.*

platform. There would be nine or ten men per engine, including the driver.

In addition to the main engine there were several other vehicles, including tenders for extra equipment. One of these was the 'dual-purpose appliance', which was a manual pump, often carrying an extending ladder or escape on large-diameter wheels, of a type still used in certain areas. When travelling to a fire the wheels of the escape were raised about two feet clear of the road. Units known as 'chemical engines' were used from the 1890s, some of them converted from obsolete hand-manual engines. The chemical engine, often dashing ahead of the steam pump, which might be delayed in the search for water or by mechanical faults, was a large copper cylinder on four wheels, with extra hose and ladders. It was a strongly reinforced vehicle with mail-coach hubs and axles and a sturdy rear platform, crewed by six men and drawn by two horses.

Horses used by the London Fire Brigade were hired to the service by Thomas Tilling of Peckham, at one time the largest job master, or provider of horses for commercial purposes, in the world. Grey horses were the rule in London, while in the provinces colour appears to have been less important, although most authorities preferred a good match. At brigade headquarters or outlying stations, horses were stabled in pairs, their harness hanging directly above them and lowered into position at the sounding of the alarm. This was specially made harness, much stronger yet lighter than other types, and also easier to adjust. There were no hip straps, cart or pad saddles, breeching or bellybands. Direct pull was through single traces from the neck collar to horizontal bars (swingletrees) on the engine. A strap connecting the neck collar with the traces, on the shoulders or withers, had a double row of bells that sounded a noisy warning when the horses moved at speed.

## Ambulances

Horse-drawn ambulances tended to be rather makeshift until the end of the nineteenth century, although some four-wheeled cabs could be converted into ambulances or ambulance-type vehicles. These were frequently fitted with solid rubber or pneumatic tyres to cushion the patient over uneven sets or cobbles. The military authorities pioneered the development of later horse-drawn ambulances, beginning with a low-slung, hooded vehicle on two wheels, and ending with a wide range of ambulance wagons on four wheels, most of the latter having full underlock.

Ambulances were also used for the transport of sick horses and other livestock, both in military and civil life. These were two-wheeled, panel-sided carts with cranked axles, very similar to the general-purpose float, but with much higher sides. The tailboard was lowered in the form of a slatted ramp, while the sick or injured horse, unable to bear its own weight, might be suspended in a body-sling let down from iron hoops. Other hoops would support a canvas or tarpaulin cover. There were both single and double ambulances, mostly drawn by a single horse, although the military version also had an outrigger or side gear for an extra horse working alongside the one between the shafts. The driver could either ride one of these horses or drive from a raised side seat,

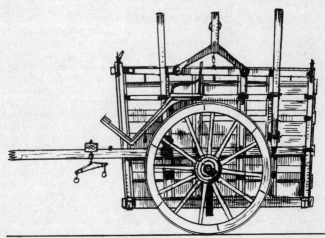

*Fig. 29. Horse ambulance.*

*Fig. 30. Tumbler cart, late nineteenth century.*

perched directly over the near-side wheel. Such vehicles were once familiar at racecourses and were used by the military at least until halfway through the Second World War.

**Vehicles used for refuse collection and street cleaning**

Local authorities used many horse-drawn vehicles to keep the roads clean and dispose of refuse. There were also water carts and wagons with sprinkler devices, some fitted with revolving brushes.

A standard vehicle for collecting street sweepings and household refuse was the four-wheeled **refuse wagon**. This was a tipping vehicle first used by the London boroughs during the 1860s, eventually becoming widespread in most urban areas. Typical features were high-panelled sides, a curved frontboard painted with the name of the local authority, small front wheels and full underlock. The colour scheme in most areas was bright red for wheels, shafts and headboard, while the rest of the bodywork was a shade of buff.

A covered **dust cart** or wagon was used during the period between the world wars, eventually mounted on pneumatic tyres. The prototype had disc wheels with solid rubber tyres. It usually had end or side tipping gear. The top was of semicircular or 'D' section, with shutters or sliding lids over the rubbish compartments of the interior. Vehicles for refuse collection were led at walking pace rather than driven. A fully loaded dust or rubbish wagon might have been up to three tons capacity, needing strong, heavy horses of the Shire type. These were known as vestry horses, their use and upkeep being controlled by the local council at 'vestry meetings', so called because they were originally held in the vestry of a church or parish hall.

What were known as **tumbler carts** may have been used for the disposal of road sweepings and sewage, especially in country areas with garden cesspits. The body of the vehicle was made from wrought iron plates and carried between two large wheels. This was a fully reinforced and watertight container, suspended on a central axle. When the top or lid was removed the body could be tipped backwards by means of a rack and pinion device attached to the shafts. There were three types or sizes, all with curved shafts, each drawn by a single horse, holding between 150 and 280 gallons as a maximum load.

The standard **water cart**, necessary for washing down streets, especially in summer, could also be used by farmers for distributing liquid manure on the land. The square tank or body of the cart or wagon was made from cemented iron plates and fitted both with a hand-manual pump and with a sprinkler or spread board or pipe, the latter midway between tank and street level. The spread board, about six feet long by a foot wide, was directly behind the rear wheels, jets of water springing from its many apertures as the vehicle moved forward. Earlier types had a man walking alongside working a pump handle, but later types were driven from a high box-seat raised on straight or curved irons. Small-sized water tanks would hold up to 120 gallons, while the larger types held between 200 and 300 gallons. An average or large-sized vehicle was the most popular for city streets, with a capacity of 270 gallons, and having a spread pipe rather than a spread board.

From the late 1850s many urban authorities and corporations used a four-wheeled vehicle known as a **road-breaker.** This was before the days of pneumatic drills driven by air-compressors and saved a great deal of time and labour with pick and shovel in breaking up old road surfaces before relaying could commence. The road-breaker was a panel-sided wagon, loaded with stones or scrap metal, and drawn by a team of four or six heavy horses. The front wheels could turn in full underlock, having iron tyres and naves. The rear wheels were large and cumbersome, usually of the dished pattern, but furnished with a double row of conical iron spikes. The team was led, rather than driven, and moved forward at a ponderous rate, breaking up the paved surface as it went. This work was later taken over by the 'scarifiers' of steam rollers, so that road-breakers were seldom seen after the 1890s. In profile the vehicle resembled a hermaphrodite, the forecarriage being

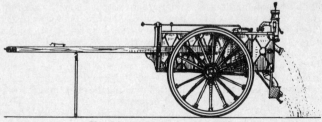

*Fig. 31. Iron water cart, 1880.*

*Fig. 32. Parcels van (GPO 'mail van').*

detachable. The wheel horses were often attached by means of double shafts rather than pole gear. The harness of leading pairs was attached to the ends of the shafts by chains.

## Royal Mail vehicles

The mails were originally carried by postboys riding horses, rather like the pony express of the old West. During the second half of the eighteenth century, however, John Palmer, an actor-manager of Bath, planned a system of mail-coaches that became a byword for safety and reliability, continuing in operation for about seventy years. These were eventually replaced by railways, although in districts beyond the railhead, or where railway services were some distance from the nearest town or village, there would be a service of horse-drawn mail vans and carts. Some of these would also bring mail to the main-line stations from the sorting offices. In remote areas of the West of England there were two-wheeled pony or donkey carts, mainly open, while larger gig-type vehicles and four-wheelers were frequently used for local collections in the larger towns.

A standard vehicle widely used from the 1880s, often travelling overnight, was the **parcel mail van,** hired by the General Post Office from the firm of McNamara. This was a closed or box van with a flat roof and a roof rack reached by a vertical ladder on the near side, placed just behind the rear wheels. There was a double box-seat on or near roof level, with large headlamps on either side of the driver's footboard. Slightly smaller side lamps were placed just above the front wheels. Each van was drawn by a team of four horses and frequently referred to as a 'mail-coach', although no passengers were carried. A horse-drawn mail van ran between London and Chatham until the summer of 1908, although it is difficult to imagine why this should have supplemented an excellent and frequent train service. There were at least half a dozen such mail-van routes out of London until 1909, one extending as far as Oxford.

During the period of the Second World War horse-drawn vans were revived by the Post Office, especially in London, to save petrol. These were for strictly local work and resembled four-wheeled bread vans, but painted in the smart livery of the GPO. They were drawn by single horses of the cob type. Most of them had pneumatic tyres and motorcar wheels. Some survived until the early 1950s.

### The hearse

The mystique of a large-scale funeral was an essential part of Victorian life, affecting all groups of society but having an almost morbid fascination for the more affluent sections of the middle and lower classes. One of the main features was an impressive cortege headed by a glass-sided hearse and followed by large numbers of closed carriages. The horses drawing the hearse were black stallions with proudly arched necks, imported from Holland and Belgium and known to the undertakers as the 'black brigade'.

The standard type of hearse, dating from the 1850s, was oblong, glass-sided and mounted on four wheels. It was driven from a high box-seat with an elaborate fringed cloth, known as a hammercloth. In some cases, however, what seemed to be cloth was merely an imitation made of carved wood. The average tare weight of such vehicles was about seventeen hundredweights and thus fairly light for a pair of good horses, although some

*Fig. 33. Hearse, 1870.*

undertakers in poorer districts used a single horse between shafts. The flat top of the vehicle would be ornamented with black ostrich plumes, usually one at each corner and a spray in the centre. Each vehicle would have full underlock and a hand-lever brake acting on the rear wheels. The forecarriage was mounted on elliptical leaf springs and the rear part of the bodywork on elliptical or semi-elliptical springs.

At one period, from the 1880s, there was also an 'elliptical hearse' with near-equirotal wheels, the underside of the bodywork based on a canoe-shape similar to a canoe-landau. Side windows were of elliptical rather than oblong dimensions. This type, however, seems to have been more popular in the United States of America than in Britain. Access to all vehicles would be through double glass doors at the rear. A few vehicles were slightly bow-shaped at the front.

**Prison vans**

The four-wheeled enclosed van, used to take prisoners to and from prisons and police courts, had barred rear and/or side windows, a rear step with grab handles and side rails.

Called a black Maria after the young Queen Victoria, known to the cockneys as 'Ria', the prototype van was introduced during the early part of her reign and had the royal monogram on either side of the bodywork. A version of this grim vehicle, in the Bath Carriage Museum, appears not unlike a large bread van. It was driven to a pair of horses and has a semi-enclosed driving seat with oval, barred windows at the sides. The small but sturdy forewheels could turn in full underlock and are mounted on fully elliptical leaf springs, while the rear bodywork is mounted on semi-elliptical springs. There are unglazed, barred windows on either side of the body, fairly small and just below the rain strip of the flat roof. There is a screw-down brake on the offside of the slatted front platform, fixed to the framework of the body by cast iron brackets. Two rails or bars on either side of the vehicle act as supports for extra police, called out to a riot, the handrail at the top being at roof level, while a lower footrail is about six inches above the rear wheels. There is a downward-sloping canopy over the front platform and dashboard. This type of vehicle was used in some districts until the early 1920s.

An alternative version of the black Maria was similar in many respects but was driven from a high box-seat and had a shorter wheelbase. There was a clerestory section of the roof, while the only windows were set in the rear doors.

**Lifeboat carriages**

These were similar to a type of military vehicle used by the Royal Engineers to transport pontoons for temporary bridging purposes. They had large artillery-type wheels and a long wheelbase; the lifeboat was cradled on bolsters between rear and forecarriages. Forewheels were slightly smaller than rear wheels, able to turn in half-lock. A team of heavy horses was needed, with chains rather than traces, drawing the carriage out to sea until the boat could be slipped or floated off on the swell.

## Bulk tankers

These were seen in both town and country, mainly from the late 1890s to the early 1920s. A number were used, during the 1900s, by large oil and petrol companies. They could be adapted, however, for any type of bulk liquid, from water to paraffin.

They were usually driven to a pair of horses and had a double box-seat with footboard and dashboard slightly in advance of the forecarriage. The driving seat was sometimes protected by a solid or folding hood or canopy but was frequently open. The general structure of the vehicle consisted of a circular, horizontal tank with top-fillers, mounted between latitudinal beams or members forming a still. There were large wheels at the rear and much smaller wheels at the front, the latter having full underlock. A shelf-like tray with side rails, for small cans, was fixed on either side of the tank, just above the level of the rear wheels. Most vehicles would have either lever or pedal brakes.

## The bathing machine

This was a tall box-like vehicle with a rear entrance reached by an inclined step-ladder. It had high clearance above water or

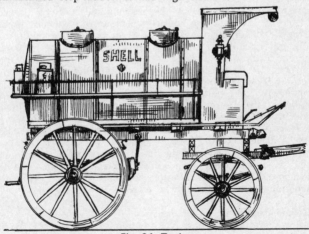

*Fig. 34. Tanker.*

ground level and was unsprung, mounted on large wheels. The roof was usually round or bow-topped for extra headroom. From a distance such vehicles resembled a clumsy type of gypsy living van or vardo.

Each vehicle was drawn out to sea by a single horse, using either chains or traces, but occasionally a pair of shafts. Front wheels were slightly smaller than back wheels but the vehicle was seldom turned, horse and gear merely changing ends for the return journey.

## The totter's cart or dray

This is a flat, dray-type vehicle, similar to the hawker's cart previously mentioned, but with a shorter wheelbase and a driving seat raised on curved or straight irons above the front wheels. Although the front wheels were formerly much smaller than those at the back, the majority are now equirotal and fitted with pneumatic tyres. The underbody of the vehicle is mounted on elliptical or semi-elliptical leaf springs, while the shafts are usually curved. Previously used by the costermongers and street traders of London, they are now mainly concerned with the collection of scrap metal and second-hand goods. Those found in other areas, especially in the Midlands and industrial North of England, are often without a driving seat.

With most commercial vehicles, wheels tend to be smaller in the northern areas of Britain than in the South and South-east.

## The vehicles of showmen

Specialised vehicles were widely used by fairground and circus showmen during the second half of the nineteenth century, although these were drawn by traction engines, rather than by horses, from the late 1890s. Most beast cages were large oblong vehicles with bars on both sides that could be protected by external shutters. The wheels were equirotal, of small diameter, and the driving seat or box was at roof level. Such vehicles would be used by circus and menagerie to provide a home on wheels for the more exotic and dangerous animals, although camels and elephants were expected not only to walk but to play their part as beasts of draught and burden. Some showmen would tour the country with a wagonload of small cages arranged in tiers on a conventional four-wheeled dray or trolley, rather like a modern hen battery. These would contain such creatures as monkeys, parrots and even fighting cocks, displayed at fairs or on village greens as a miniature zoo, the owner collecting money from spectators by passing round the hat.

Generally, vehicles for travelling shows were drawn by one or more horses, sometimes harnessed in teams. Many were constructed by the firm of Savage and Company of King's Lynn, specialising in both fairground and agricultural equipment. There were both open and closed wagons, the former mainly used for beams, props, poles and rounding boards, while the latter, containing more precious and fragile items such as the horses for the roundabout, were known in the trade as 'horse trucks'. Even the centre-engines and mechanical organs for the 'rides' were mounted on four-wheeled carriages, each drawn by two or more horses. At one period Savages produced a steam-powered generating set, for electric lighting, on a four-wheeled truck.

Many of the showmen had elaborate living vans, known as **Burton vans,** of a type first constructed at Burton-on-Trent. These were four-wheeled and panel-sided, similar to many used by the Romany people, but having equirotal or near-equirotal wheels. The genuine gypsy living van or vardo had much larger wheels at the back than the front, the rear wheels being at the sides rather than below the bodywork. While the wagons of showmen usually kept to the main roads, gypsy vans were equally at home on the open heath or down rutted lanes and side tracks, a poor road requiring larger wheels than a flat or paved surface.

In later years the wealthier showmen preferred an even larger living van, known as the **saloon type.** This had a longer wheelbase than the Burton van and smaller wheels in proportion to its size, eventually furnished with pneumatic tyres. Although often finishing as part of a road train drawn by a motor vehicle or traction engine the original versions were hauled by one or more

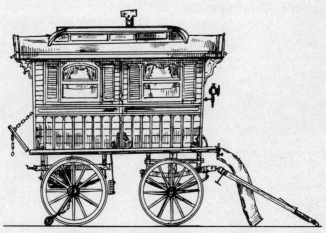

*Fig. 35. Showman's living van, 1890s.*

horses. The entrance, reached by steps from ground level, was often at the side, rather than front or back. The windows, above waist level, had elaborate panes of frosted or cut glass, while side panels would be lined out with gold leaf. Interiors would be furnished with free-standing tables, beds and chairs rather than the end-bunks and built-in equipment of smaller caravans. Both the Burton and saloon vans would have clerestory roofs.

# 5. American types

Perhaps the most outstanding of the early vehicles used by settlers in North America was the **Conestoga wagon,** associated with long treks over the prairies. This was the original covered wagon or prairie schooner, although first designed as an ordinary farm or commercial wagon for use in the Conestoga valley, Pennsylvania, about 1755. Its high sides and canvas top, projecting fore and aft, made it an ideal temporary home, while its construction was so sturdy that it could cope with almost any terrain. The vehicle was solid and unsprung with panel sides, some later types also having hand-lever brakes acting on the rear wheels. The large forewheels were allowed only a short or limited lock. There was an average of ten hoops to support the canvas top. Some wagons in the early days were drawn by oxen but most had a team of six or four horses.

There was a wide range of both two-wheeled and four-wheeled vehicles used from the colonial days until the twentieth century. They frequently had a longer wheelbase than British types, while there were less obvious distinctions between those needed for farmwork and commercial vehicles on the city streets. Carts were less frequently seen than wagons and mainly preferred in the southern states for light work on plantations. These were **dump** or **tip carts,** frequently drawn by a small horse or mule, and used in the northern states by builders and contractors. The latter type was usually plank- or straight-sided to the height of one or two planks. Most carts would automatically dump when unhooked at the front end. A two-wheeled coal cart, mainly used in small towns of the East and country districts, resembled a version of the scotch cart and was of one ton capacity.

Four-wheeled wagons used by farmers, contractors and plantation owners were of three or four main types, with either equirotal or near-equirotal wheels, large in proportion to the size of the vehicle, and constructed for work over rough tracks and badly made roads. A small **spring wagon** with a shallow or tray-like body and full-lock or 'cut-under' forecarriage was used for light haulage. A **one-horse farm wagon,** of a type still being manufactured in fair numbers, was a low-slung oblong or tray-shaped vehicle with a box-seat on either transverse or crosswise

*Fig. 36. American farm wagon, 1900.*

springs (nutcracker springs), about eighteen inches from the frontboard.

At one time the motorcar-manufacturing firm of Studebaker made a wide range of horse-drawn vehicles, both short-lock and cut-under types, culminating in the specially made **Studebaker wagon,** drawn by a pair of horses, that won many awards and medals at international exhibitions. There was also a Studebaker military wagon of a similar design, used up to the period of the First World War. The civilian version was near-equirotal, having quarter lock, hand-lever brakes and draught from a centre-pole. Compared with the average American wagon, it was high-sided with a high centre of gravity, being about twelve feet in length.

A low-sided **mountain wagon** was frequently used in highland districts. This had what was known as a rack bed of lateral members and could be used for hauling timber. It was further noted for large, heavy brake blocks acting on the rear wheels.

In towns and cities there were large numbers of drays and wagons with stake sides, used to convey barrels, casks and bales. These were either dead-axle or sprung vehicles, many used by brewers for street deliveries. Timber carriages, in both town and country, were usually known as **log trucks** or **lumber buggies,** similar to those used in Britain but often with larger wheels. Pipes, lengths of timber and sometimes girders were hauled on articulated or limbered gear, similar to the timber carriage but with high corner posts at front and back, to keep the load steady.

The **ice wagon** was a once familiar sight in the city streets, and there were two main versions. The smaller and more popular type had a cut-under forecarriage, high sides, a high box-seat and an ample rear step with grab handles, for access to the interior. This could be either an open or a covered vehicle, driven to one or two

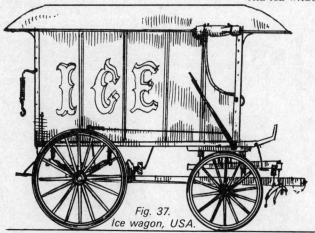

Fig. 37.
Ice wagon, USA.

horses, and with a capacity of two tons. The interior was equipped with ice-hooks, racks and scales. An even larger type, always drawn by two horses, with a fixed top and rear canopy, had a semi-enclosed driving seat with side windows rather than an open box.

The **transfer dray** was a long, flat, open vehicle with raised backboard and high box-seat. This was used for conveying, among other things, theatrical scenery and rolls of newsprint. It was usually drawn by a pair of heavy horses harnessed to a centre-pole.

The city **coal wagon** was a large, four-wheeled vehicle, having a wooden outer-body lined with iron sheeting. There was a single box-seat at the centre-front on elliptical springs, with a small footboard. Capacity was two and a half tons, and the wagon was drawn by two horses.

There were many versions of the **delivery van or wagon** and **tradesman's cart,** especially from the 1890s. These were mainly well sprung and driven from either an inner enclosed seat or an open box-seat. Perhaps the most outstanding was the **milk wagon** for delivering bottled milk. This had a step-in middle section with sliding doors on either side of a cut-under forecarriage. The rear body was mounted on transverse springs, while the forecarriage was mounted on both lateral springs and crosswise springs, united by 'D' links. There was a small front platform under a canopy, on which crates of empties could be stacked. Above the waistline of the vehicle were several square windows of plain or frosted glass, there being either eight or six at the sides and two at the front.

The **baker's wagon,** an equivalent of the English bread van, had a long wheelbase, near-equirotal wheels and half-lock on the forecarriage. The rear was mounted on fully elliptical side springs

*Fig. 38. Milk wagon, 1910.*

and the fore part on a single elliptical cross spring. There were sliding side panels and drop windows, also an outward-opening door on each side of the enclosed driving position.

The **butcher's wagon** was drawn by a pair of horses, harnessed to a centre-pole. It usually had double windows at the front and side doors, with an enclosed driving position. The interior was boarded to the waistline and the upper parts were lined with white cotton duck. There was also a rear canopy or hood and a slatted floor.

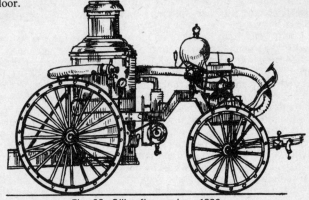

*Fig. 39. Silby fire-engine, 1880.*

The North American horse-drawn steam **fire-engine** was constructed on arched irons with full cut-under of the forecarriage. There were four main types, the 'Gould', 'Button', 'Silby' and 'Amoskeag', the last being much larger than the first three and favoured by the New York City Fire Department. Apart from the driving seat, boiler, pump and hose-rack, these vehicles were merely carrying frames. The firemen rode on a following tender, with spare hose and ladders.

Britain and America, as the foremost commercial nations of the nineteenth century, set the fashion in most types of horse-drawn vehicles, especially from the 1860s. Many cities in five continents had vehicles of both British and American type, according to their business affiliations and spheres of influence.

# 6. Features and methods of construction

Heavier commercial and utility vehicles were based on the evolution of wagons, used by both carriers and farmers, while lighter vehicles were more akin to the later design of carriages.

The bodywork of the traditional wagon was carried on a framework or bed of wooden lengthwise and cross members. This

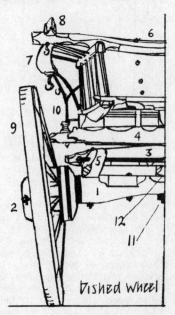

Fig. 40. Front elevation of a traditional wagon: 1 axletree, 2 nave, 3 bolster, 4 pillow, 5 hound, 6 front rail, 7 and 8 outer rails, 9 tyre, 10 side support, 11 king pin, 12 coupling pole.

Dished wheel

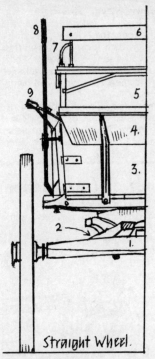

Fig. 41. Front elevation of unsprung light wagon: 1 axletree, 2 futchels, 3 frontboard, 4 footboard, 5 box-seat, 6 back rail, 7 guard irons, 8 brake lever, 9 raves or sideboards.

Straight Wheel.

in turn had an **underperch** or coupling pole in the form of a lateral beam connecting fore and hind carriages. **Bolsters** or cross beams lay between the bodywork and the perch, also resting on the axletrees. Parallel members projecting forward from the front of the wagon, known as **hounds** or **futchels,** connected with the draught gear — either shafts or a crossbar (splinter bar) — to which traces could be attached for use with a centre-pole. A king pin through the centre of perch, bolster and axletree enabled the forewheels to turn in part or full lock, later wagons having a wheel-like plate or turntable.

The **axle,** usually made by specialists — both individual craftsmen and manufacturing firms, had arms on either side of the axletree, reinforced with iron wearing plates, although later made entirely of iron or steel. For dished wheels of the concave type, invented during the sixteenth century but widely introduced a century later, the axle arms were turned slightly downwards. The **dished wheel,** claimed to give better support to a heavy load on

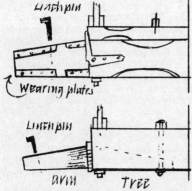

Fig. 42. Wooden axletrees: (above) with wooden arm; (below) with iron arm.

rough surfaces, had the spokes set at an obtuse angle to the hub so that a cross-section of the wheel appeared as a cone. Spokes and parts of the framework of a wooden wagon were shaved, trimmed or chamfered, not only for decorative effect but to decrease overall weight.

Lighter vehicles intended to travel at faster speeds over better roads, from the end of the eighteenth century, were mounted on **elbow or 'C' springs** and later on elliptical or semi-elliptical **leaf springs,** as with carriages and coaches. Leaf springs were the most widely used, after their introduction in 1804, until the present century. They allowed the vehicle builder to eliminate the underperch, although this was sometimes replaced by iron bars within — or reinforcing — the underframe. In effect the support of leaf springs identified the body of carriage, wagon or van with its own underperch.

The **axle** of a light vehicle was a single through rod of iron,

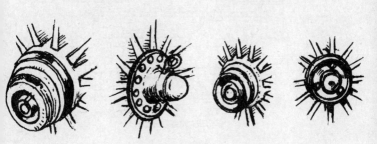

Fig. 43. Hubs or naves : (from left) wagon type, artillery, collinge, mail-coach.

although sometimes protected by a wooden axle case. Wheels for all types of vehicle were either straight or dished, a matter of controversy for over three centuries. **Hubs** and **naves** or wheel centres were of wood and/or iron, the two main forms for lighter vehicles being the mail-coach hub and the collinge. The mail-coach hub and wheel, of great strength and reliability, were first used in connection with early mail-coaches but were later adapted for many other types of vehicle. The wheel was secured to the hub by three large bolts passing through a plate into the nave or surrounding wheel-stock. This was the safest hub/axle ever invented, as all three bolts had to snap at the same time for the wheel to come off — a near impossibility. The collinge type of hub was a useful alternative on lighter vehicles, this being conical and funnel-shaped, held in place by a centre nut. Cheaper, wooden hubs were secured by stock hoops or nave bands, shrunk on to the stocks.

**Tyres** were at first iron strips or strakes applied in sections, replacing heavy nails or studs. These were replaced in turn by band tyres, shrunk on to the wheel when heated. The band tyre was invented in 1767, but strakes remained in use, especially for larger wagons in country districts (where they may have been easier to replace) until the late nineteenth century. Solid rubber tyres and later pneumatic tyres were introduced towards the end of the nineteenth century, mainly to decrease the noise of heavy wheels on cobbles or sets. They were widely used on both commercial and agricultural vehicles during the 1930s, although

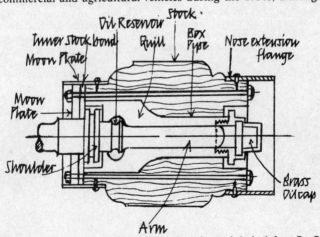

Fig. 44. Cross-section of mail-coach axle and hub (after B. B. Murdock).

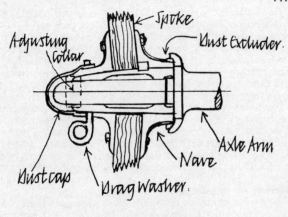

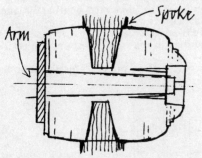

*Fig. 45. Cross-section of artillery hub (top) and cart or wagon hub.*

often increasing the weight of the vehicle. Their use is still a matter of controversy, although it is certain that they appeared less attractive than iron-shod wheels.

**Brakes** were mainly either hand-lever or foot-pedal types, connected to the wooden or metal blocks of the rear wheels by rod or wire. They were not widely used until the second half of the nineteenth century, most vehicles on inclines depending on drag shoe and roller scotch to defy gravity. Screw-down brakes were mainly used to prevent a runaway when vehicles were left unattended.

Two-wheeled carts with shafts had **prop-sticks** attached on the underside of each shaft, which helped to take the weight of the load while the cart was delayed in a standing position.

Originally most vehicles were made by groups of craftsmen,

sharing different aspects of their work in a small yard. In later years details of the craft became highly specialised and some firms began to concentrate on certain types of vehicle, or even special parts, for which they had gained a reputation through demand and experience. During the latter part of the nineteenth century large firms in industrial areas began to take over from local craftsmen, supplying not only customers in their own region but buyers from continental Europe and the colonies. Many concerns such as the railway companies and the co-operative societies, using large numbers of vehicles, manufactured most of their own carts, wagons and vans. The smaller companies, however, often bought vehicles from large-scale producers such as the Gloster Carriage and Wagon Company, the Bristol Wagon Company and Messrs Hayes and Son of Stamford and Peterborough.

## Materials for construction

The nave or centre of a wooden wheel was made from elm, but to a lesser extent from oak or ash. This was on account of the twisted grain of elm wood that prevented splitting. In later years wheel naves and other fittings were made from iron and steel.

Spokes were made from cleft rather than sawn heart of oak, cut from the wood according to the lie of the grain, also taking care not to cross the grain.

Felloes, or the outer parts of the wheel containing the

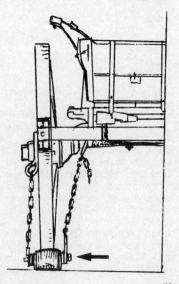

*Fig. 46. Roller scotch (arrowed).*

extremities of the spokes which radiate from the centre or hub, were made of ash, on account of its natural flexibility, Less successful felloes have also been made from beech or elm.

Metal tyres were made from iron and later steel. Some claim that steel tyres are better than iron as the latter wear less evenly and tend to flake or crack.

Axletrees of large wagons were usually made of beech. Later types had iron arms and trees of beech wood. Hounds, futchels and bolsters were made of ash or oak.

Shafts and poles were made of ash, although some shafts for lighter vehicles were made of lancewood.

The framework of the traditional wagon was made of oak, reinforced with strong ironwork. Elm planks were used for side planks and panels and floorboards, those with knots being preferred as a precaution against splitting. Side spindles were of poplar or ash. In more recent years the upper works of commercial vans have been made from a wide range of materials from plywood and aluminium to light metal alloys.

# 7. Driving and harness

Horses used in most commercial vehicles were driven from a box-seat mounted on the front or forecarriage. Some heavy wagons, however, would have their teams led on foot by men acting as guides or drovers rather than drivers.

A single horse would draw its vehicle by means of shafts, which were either straight or curved arms on either side of its body. A pair of horses, although sometimes using double shafts, were usually hitched in tandem, for carts, or on either side of a coach, wagon or van pole. The traces or chains for pole harness would lead back to a horizontal splinter bar on the front of the vehicle, although sometimes to smaller bars known as swingletrees, attached to a drawbar, the single or swingletrees united by a double tree or whippletree. Leading horses, in front of the rear or wheel horses, were harnessed with lighter, less elaborate gear to swingletrees attached to the head of the centre-pole.

There were various combinations of horse teams, the most popular being pairs (two horses, side by side), tandem (two horses, one behind the other), threes (three horses abreast, known in Russia as a troika), unicorn (two horses behind and one in front), sledge-hammer (a pair or more horses in front and a single behind), four-in-hand (one pair of horses in front and one behind) and sixes (three pairs of horses behind each other). There was no upper limit and there were many permutations for heavy and awkward loads, especially in the United States and Canada. Teams of more than six, however, had to be specially trained and were usually driven for show, as in circus parades and carnivals.

A Barnum and Bailey circus wagon was once noted for its forty-horse hitch, recreated about sixty years later by the Schlitz Brewing Company, at a parade organised by the Baraboo Circus Museum (Wisconsin) in 1972.

The main function of harness was to attach the horse to the vehicle or to other members of the team, and also to provide a measure of direct control for the driver. Straps, traces and chains form attachments while the main pull was at the fore end of the horse by means of neck or breast collar and harness. Both types had obvious advantages and disadvantages, although the neck collar was widely used in Britain and better suited than the breast collar to the conformation of the average British draught horse. Great care, however, had to be taken in fitting the neck collar to avoid galls and discomfort, especially in hot climates, making it less suitable for military harness than the breast collar. In the latter case a dead or badly injured horse might have to be replaced in a team at short notice, and the lengthy routine of collar fitting would prove irksome and dangerous. While breast collars and harness proved easier to adjust in the field allowing greater

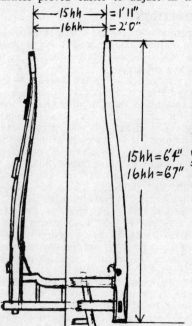

15hh ⟶ = 1'11"
16hh ⟶ = 2'0"

15hh = 6'4"
16hh = 6'7"

*Fig. 47. Shafts are normally symmetrical. The example left is a half set for a small vehicle and horse, the example right for a larger, heavier vehicle and horse. The measurements refer to the length of shaft and width between the shafts suitable for horses 15 and 16 hands high (hh).*

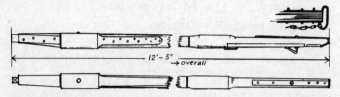

*Fig. 48. Wagon pole : (top right) alternative head of pole; (centre) elevation; (bottom) plan.*

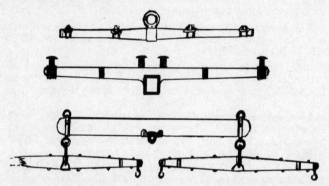

*Fig. 49. (Top) Pole bar. (Centre) Splinter bar. (Bottom) Whippletree and swingletrees.*

freedom of movement, the neck collar proved more suitable for heavier loads at slower paces in civil life.

The breeching of harness was an arrangement of broad straps on the hindquarters of a horse, useful in holding back the load on a downward gradient, but was not always used with light horses attached to smaller two-wheeled vehicles.

The crupper or looped tail strap was mainly used for keeping the tail down and to prevent it getting mixed up with the reins, which might hamper control. For the latter reason many draught horses were docked (their tails cut short), although this is now forbidden by law.

Nearly all draught horses wore blinkers or side shields on the upper part of their bridles, to prevent them catching a glimpse of the revolving wheels from the corners of their eyes, which sometimes caused them to bolt. This, however, only happened with very young or badly broken horses, blinkers being less widely used in military circles and on the continent of Europe. As with docked tails, however, they soon became a fashion rather than a necessity.

# 8. Where to see horse-drawn commercial vehicles

**Acton Scott Working Farm Museum,** Wenlock Lodge, Acton Scott, Church Stretton, Shropshire SY6 6QN. Telephone: Marshbrook (069 46) 306. Horse-drawn vehicles and implements of a traditional type are used daily.

**American Museum in Britain,** Claverton Manor, Bath, Avon BA2 7BD. Telephone: Bath (0225) 60503. The collection includes a Conestoga wagon of pioneer days.

**Bass Museum of Brewing History,** Horninglow Street, Burton on Trent, Staffordshire. Telephone: Burton on Trent (0283) 42031. Brewers' delivery drays.

**Bath Carriage Museum,** Circus Mews, Bath, Avon. Telephone: Bath (0225) 25175. Mainly pleasure and private carriages but the collection also includes a police van and a horse-drawn hearse.

**Birmingham Museum of Science and Industry,** Newhall Street, Birmingham B3 1RZ. Telephone: 021-236 1022. Horse-drawn Shand Mason fire engine with a steam powered pump, c 1898.

**Black Country Museum,** Tipton Road, Dudley, West Midlands DY1 4SQ. Telephone: 021-557 9643. A number of horse-drawn vehicles associated with the Black Country.

**Blakesley Hall,** Blakesley Road, Yardley, Birmingham B25 8RN. Telephone: 021-783 2193. Displays a fine carrier's cart, c 1890, a farm tip cart and a horse-drawn baker's van of the Hovis pattern.

**Bristol Industrial Museum,** Prince's Wharf, Bristol, Avon BS1 4RN. Telephone: Bristol (0272) 299771, extension 290. A collection of horse-drawn vehicles including the pioneer caravan 'The Wanderer.'

**Courage Shire Horse Centre,** Maidenhead Thicket, near Maidenhead, Berkshire SL6 3QD. Telephone: Littlewick Green (062 882) 3917.

**Glasgow Museum of Transport,** 25 Albert Drive, Glasgow G41 2PE. Telephone: 041-423 8000. An interesting collection of horse-drawn vehicles of all types.

**Guinness Museum,** St James's Gate Brewery, Dublin 8, Eire. Telephone: 01 756701. Collection of vehicles connected with the delivery of Guinness stout.

**Hereford and Worcester County Museum,** Hartlebury Castle, Hartlebury, near Kidderminster, Worcestershire DY11 7XZ. Telephone: Hartlebury (0299) 250416. The collection includes farm and delivery vehicles and living vans formerly owned by showmen and Romany folk. There is a hearse and a horse-drawn ambulance.

**Leicestershire Museum of Technology,** Abbey Pumping Station, Corporation Road, Abbey Lane, Leicester. Telephone: Leicester (0533) 661330. A selection of commercial horse-drawn vehicles including a horse bus and a fire engine. Vehicles on display are regularly exchanged with those in store. Those in store may be viewed by appointment.

**Melton Carneigie Museum,** Thorpe End, Melton Mowbray, Leicestershire. Telephone: Melton Mowbray (0664) 69946. A selection of horse-drawn vehicles including a baker's van.

**Museum of East Anglian Life,** Stowmarket, Suffolk IP14 1DL. Telephone: Stowmarket (0449) 612229. Farm and commercial vehicles associated with East Anglia.

**North of England Open Air Museum,** Beamish, near Stanley, County Durham. Telephone: Stanley (0207) 231811. A selection of commercial and agricultural vehicles, including the last horse-drawn Ringtons tea van. It is also the home of the Newcastle Breweries dray horses.

**Science Museum,** Exhibition Road, South Kensington, London SW7 2DD. Telephone: 01-589 3456. One of the largest of all national transport collections, but only a few examples are on display at any one time. Scale models explain the development of horse transport through the ages. Interesting model of a dead horse cart.

**Solid Fuel Advisory Service, Shire Horse Stables,** The Shires Estate, Birmingham Road, Lichfield, Staffordshire. Telephone: Lichfield (054 32) 52809. The stables of the Shire horse team are open to the public and the horses, vehicles, harness and tack are on display. The horses deliver fuel within the local area and appear in carnivals and festivals.

**Tyrwhitt-Drake Museum of Carriages,** Archbishop's Stables, Mill Street, Maidstone, Kent. Telephone: Maidstone (0622) 54497. Mainly private carriages but one or two commercial vehicles.

**Yorkshire Museum of Carriages and Horse-drawn Vehicles,** Yore Mill, Aysgarth Falls, Aysgarth, Leyburn, North Yorkshire. Telephone: Richmond (0748) 3275. Nearly fifty horse-drawn vehicles of all types including a wool dray, fire engines, butchers' and bakers' carts, a furniture pantechnicon, hansom cab, milk floats and many other trade vehicles.

# Glossary

**Axle or Axle arm:** Spindle on which a wheel turns.

**Axletree:** There are two main forms: in one the spindle is supported by a wooden beam, and in the other the wheels are attached to either end of the beam.

**Box:** Raised seat from which a vehicle is driven.

**Chamfer:** The shaving or carving of the spokes and framework of a vehicle to lighten the weight.

**Colletts:** Metal bands or washers used for securing the hub on certain types of wheel.

**Dashboard:** Raised frontboard in advance of the driving seat.

**Dish:** Special type of wheel set at an angle and having an arrangement of concave spokes.

**Equirotal:** Of a four-wheeled vehicle, with all wheels of equal size.

**Felloes, Fellies:** Sections of a wheel rim to which spokes are fitted by means of a tongue or tenon.

**Footboard:** Raised board at the front of a driving seat or box, used to support the feet. Usually at an angle of forty-five degrees and fronted by a dashboard.

**Futchels:** Prong-like parts of the forecarriage to which draught gear may be attached.

**Headed:** Covered with a roof or top.

**Hermaphrodite:** A compromise vehicle between a cart and a wagon, having a detachable forecarriage.

**Hound:** Lateral supporting member on the forecarriage of a wagon.

**Leaf springs:** Steel springs made from elliptical or semi-elliptical plates or leaves, usually several in number. These are attached to the bodywork or undercarriage by 'scroll-irons' or strong metal loops.

**Ladder:** Rack-like support attached to either front or tailboard of a harvest wagon to support an overhanging load.

**Lock:** Angle through which forewheels of a vehicle turn.

**Nave:** The centre of a wheel or hub.

**Perch:** Also an underperch. Bar or frame supporting the underbody of a vehicle. Also an attachment between fore and hind carriages.

**Pole:** Centre bar to which a pair of horses may be harnessed, one on either side.

**Prop-stick:** Stick or bar used to support the shafts of a cart.

**Rim:** Outer part of a wheel, next to the tyre.

**Roller bolt:** Used to fasten or attach the traces of pole harness.

**Skid pan:** Metal shoe or wedge, known in some country districts as a drug bat. Fits under the nearside rear wheel of a heavy four-wheeled vehicle, to serve as a crude brake.

**Spindles:** Vertical supports for the sides of a wagon or cart.

**Splinter bar:** Cross beam on the forecarriage to which shafts, pole or swingletree may be fitted.

**Swingletree:** Horizontal bar to which harness traces or chains may be attached on certain types of vehicle, there being a bar for each horse.

**Tyre or Tire:** Metal band, either iron or steel, fitted to the outer rim of a wheel. Later replaced by a solid rubber or pneumatic tyre.

**Wheel plates:** Circular iron plates bolted under the forecarriage on which the wheels of a vehicle turn.

**Whippletree:** An attachment for draught gear, fixed to the forecarriage of a vehicle.

# Bibliography

Bird, Anthony. *Roads and vehicles*. Longman Green. 1969.

Edwards, Lionel. *Thy servant the horse*. Country Life. 1952.

James, Arnold. *Farm waggons of England and Wales*. John Baker. 1969.

Jenkins, J. Geraint. *The English farm wagon*. Oakwood Press, for the University of Reading. 1961.

Lang, Jennifer. *An assemblage of nineteenth century horse drawn carriages*. Perpetua Press. 1971. (Containing illustrations of many commercial vehicles from the original sketches by William Francis Freelove.)

Rittenhouse, Jack D. *American horse drawn vehicles*. Crown Publishers, New York. 1958.

Smith, D. J. *Discovering horse-drawn carriages*. Shire Publications. 1985.

Sturt, George (George Bourne). *The wheelwright's shop*. Cambridge University Press. 1923. (Paperback edition, 1963.)

Tarr, Laszlo. *The history of carriages*. Corvina Press, Budapest. 1969. Translation by Elisabeth Hoch: Vision Press, London, 1969.

Tylden, Major G. *Discovering harness and saddlery*. Shire Publications. 1971.

Vince, John. *Discovering carts and wagons*. Shire Publications. Second edition 1974.

Ward-Jackson, C. H. and Harvey, Denis E. *The English gypsy caravan*. David and Charles. 1969.

Watney, Marylian and Watney, Sanders. *Horse power*. Hamlyn. 1975.

*Army Service Corps training. Part III: Transport*. HMSO. 1911.

# Index

Aluminium 22
Ambulances 52
Amoskeag (fire-engine) 65
Artillery wheels 32, 58
Ash (wood) 70, 71
Axle 53, 66, 67
Axle arms 66, 67
Axle case 68
Axletree 66, 67
Baker's cart 63
Bakery vehicles 20, 22
Band tyre 68
Barge wagon 11
Barnum and Bailey 72
Bathing machines 58, 59
Battery lamps 32
Black brigade 56
Black Maria 57
Blinkers 73
Boat wagon 11
Boiler trolley 32
Bolsters 13, 66
Bow fronts 19
Bow wagon 11
Box seat 19, 54, 57, 71
Braithwaite and Ericsson 49
Brakes 19, 20, 23, 31, 50, 57, 61, 69
Bread vans 20
Breeching 51, 73
Brewer's dray 27
Bristol Wagon Company 70
British Railways 29
Builder's carts 17
Burton vans 60
Butcher's cart 21
Butcher's wagon 64
Butchery vehicles 21
Button (fire-engine) 65
Canoe-landau 52
Carriage truck 28
Carrier's cart 6, 10
Carrier's wagon 9, 10
Carts 4, 5, 6, 9, 12, 14, 20
Centre pole 64, 66, 71
Chamfered 4, 5
Chariots 4, 5
Clerestory roof 57, 61
Coal cart 15
Coal wagon 16, 25, 63
Cob 9, 17, 20
Collar, neck 4
Collinge 6
Conestoga wagon 61
Co-operative Societies 23
Cranked axles 11, 18, 22
Cranked wheels 32
Crossbar 6
Cross springs 64
Crupper 73
C springs 67
Dashboard 22, 25, 32, 57
Dead axle 62
Delivery vehicles 20
Dished wheels 66
D links 63

Drag shoe 20, 30
Drawbar 31, 71
Drays 6, 14, 27, 29, 31, 62
Driving 71
Drop windows 64
Dual-purpose appliance 51
Dump carts 61
Dung carts 12
Dust cart 53
Elbow springs 67
Elm (wood) 70, 71
Equirotal 22, 26, 59, 61
Equirotal wheels 28, 32
Escape (ladder) 51
Etruscans 6
Farm wagon 10, 11
Felloes 70, 71
Fire Brigade Act 49
Fire-engines 32, 49, 50, 65
Flanders wagon 8
Flap doors 71
Flemings 9
Float 18, 19, 22
Floorboards 71
Forecarriage 13, 20, 32, 54, 63, 65, 71
Frontboard 24, 25, 53
Furniture van 28
Futchels 66, 71
Gloster Wagon and Carriage Company 70
Gould (fire-engine) 65
Great Northern Railway 31
Great Western Railway 31
Greeks 6, 7
Greengrocery vehicles 23
Grocery vans 25
Gypsy van 59, 60
Hackney (pony) 26
Hadley Simpkin 49
Hammercloth 56
Harness 71, 72
Harvest wagons 11, 13
Hawker's carts 24
Hayes and Son 70
Headboard 26, 53
Headed 10
Headlamps 55
Hearse 56
Hermaphrodite 13, 54
Hoops 19, 20, 25, 52
Hop wagon (Kentish) 11
Horses 4, 12, 16, 27, 28, 29, 53, 61, 71
Horse trucks 60
Hound 66
Hub 20, 67, 68, 71
Hub brakes 32
Hub caps 24
Hybrids 29
Ice cart 28
Ice cream cart 29
Ice wagon 62
Jobbers 27
Ladders 11
Lamps 20

Lancewood 71
Laundry vans 25
Leaf springs 11, 19, 29, 30, 50, 67
Ledge sides 28
Lifeboat carriages 57
Lockers 23, 24
Log trucks 62
London Fire Brigade 51
Lorry 31
Low-loader 29, 52
Lumber buggies 62
Mail-coaches 7, 20, 55
Mail-coach hub 51, 68
Mail van 55
Manchester market cart 25
Manual pumps 49, 51
McAdam 10
McNamara 55
Metal alloys 22, 71
Metcalf 10
Middle Ages 7, 8
Midland Railway 31
Milk-delivery vehicles 22, 32
Milk wagon 63
Miller's wagon 14
Mudguards 24
Napoleonic wars 8
Nave 68, 77
Neck collar 52, 72, 73
Nutcracker springs 62
Oak (wood) 70, 71
One-horse farm wagon 61
Outrigger 52
Oxen 4, 6, 61
Palmer, John 55
Panels 25, 61
Panel-sided 14, 15, 17, 20, 28, 30, 53
Parcel vans 29, 30
Perch 8, 9, 66
Plank-sided 16
Platform 13, 16, 18
Plywood 71
Pneumatic tyres 22, 23, 24, 31, 32, 52, 56, 59, 68
Pole 71
Pole harness 71
Post Office 56
Prison vans 57
Propsticks 69
Rack and pinion 54
Railway cartage 29
Raves 28, 29
Refuse wagon 53
Renaissance 7, 9
Road-breaker 54
Road trains 28, 60
Roller scotch 20, 69
Romans 6-7
Rounding boards 28
Rubber tyres (solid) 53, 68
Rulley 31
Saloon vans 60
Savage and Company 60
Scotch cart 13, 31, 61

# INDEX

Scuttlebox dashboard 32
Shafts 4, 5, 6, 13, 25, 28, 29, 32, 49, 53, 54, 55, 57, 59, 66, 69, 71
Shand, James 50
Shand Mason 50
Sideboards 17, 18, 29, 30
Silby (fire-engine) 65
Single-horse trolley 31
Single-horse van 30
Single-horse wagon 29
Sledge 4
Sledgehammer 71
Slide car 4
Spindles 8
Spindle-sided 9, 25
Splinterbar 66, 71
Spokes 67, 71
Spreadboard 54
Spreadpipe 54
Spring cart 31
Springs 31, 63
Spring wagon 61
Stage wagons 6, 10
Stake sides 62
Step-in cart 21
Stock hoops 68

Stone cart 17, 18
Studebaker Company 62
Studebaker wagons 62
Swingletrees 51, 71
Tailboard 21, 25, 28, 52
Tandem 18, 71
Tankers 58
Tar-boilers 58
Telford, Thomas 10
Tilling, Thomas (job-master) 51
Timber bob 13
Timber carriage 13, 29, 62
Timber neb 13
Tip carts 61
Top fillers 58
Totter's cart 24, 59
Traces 71, 72
Tradesman's cart 63
Troika 71
Trolley 11, 28, 29, 31
Trouncer 27
Trulley 31
Tumbler cart 53
Tumbril 12
Turntable 66
Tyres 9, 11, 68, 71
Undercarriage 50

Underlock 11, 20, 22, 25, 29, 30, 49, 54
Underperch 11, 67
Unicorn 71
Van boy 30
Vanner 20
Van pole 71
Vans 70
Vardo 59, 60
Vestry horses 53
Wagons 4, 5, 6, 8, 14, 19, 29, 65, 70, 71
Wain 12
Waisted 11
Water-barrel carts 14
Water carts 53, 54
Welsh cob 23
Wheelbase 27
Wheels 4, 13, 68
Wheelstock 68
Wheelwright 11
Whippletree 71
Whitbread, Samuel 15
Windlass 13
Windscreen 22